Me among the STARS

A Mosaic of Broken Faith and Unexpected Hope

For privacy reasons, some names, locations, and dates may have been changed.

Paperback ISBN: 979-8-9880345-0-6

Book Cover by Stefan Proudfoot, Spiffing Covers

Unless otherwise noted, all Scripture quotations are quoted from the NASB 1995 Bible.

me among the STARS

A Mosaic of Broken Faith and Unexpected Hope

HEIDI S. TREIBEL

Dedication

To the three I see each day: You've given me wings and the courage to try. You are the ultimate inspiration and reason. Each of you is a wonder.

To the three I can only see in my spirit: You give me eyes for the unseen. Because you live, there is hope for everyone and everything. This heavy hope anchors me upward.

To my husband and best friend: We've walked and wrestled together, and no one could have loved me better through it all. I'm so grateful that our awkward first encounter turned into a lifetime together.

To my family and my friends: Every word of love, every gift of remembrance, every text, every tear, every embrace has mattered. Thank you.

This book is dedicated to this tremendous mix of beautiful people. I could never pick just one.

Acknowledgements

Thank you to the friends and family who encouraged me to turn my journal rantings and blog posts into a book. Thank you for valuing Elliot's story. Many thanks to my readers and advice-givers for your guidance in the publishing process. Thank you, Abbey, for your fabulous editing and to the team at Spiffing Covers for your invaluable help and services.

Contents

Introduction

"Mommy, can you make my dragon's face more fiercer?" My child interrupts my fixation on the wall on the other side of the alley that I had been staring at through the window. I mold the dragon's floppy clay face into some semblance of "fierce," though gravity's influence is stronger than mine. The other parents help their children with clay dragons, and we smile at each other knowingly. Sure, an art class for the "kids"—with parental fingerprints on every project. Oh well. This weekly art class at a downtown visual arts center promises an art project—without the mess in my house!

And this art studio is just cool. Not only does the staff help children of all ages create art from new materials, but they seem to revel in creating something new out of the old. Candy wrappers, plastic bottles, and toilet paper tubes hang in funky arrangements around the building, becoming silhouettes, foxes, and words. Whatever the mind's eye of an artist can envision.

Mosaic seems to be a favorite of the visionaries who create here. I never much thought about the symbolism or inherent beauty of mosaics before now. Mosaics begin with broken pieces—glass, pottery, and discarded shards of more perfect projects. Then an artist with a vision for bringing beauty out of the broken arranges these eclectic extras into something new. A walkway from the parking lot. A bench we play on after art class. A giant turtle whose shell is an array of colorful pieces of glass.

I look again to the building across the alley, also part of the art studio's property. The entire wall is a mosaic made of broken glass: swirling colors, decadent patterns, and bright innovation. A new creation made from broken pieces.

But to arrive at this beauty, what an enormous amount of shattering it must have taken. What a lot of work and time and effort on the part of the artist. And during the process, this breathtaking wall of wonder likely looked like nothing more than a big mess.

I get that. I am still a jumbled, broken mess many days. The me who once was, the me of crystal-clear faith and child-like trust, she experienced her own shattering.

That Moment

I still remember the sound of the alarm on my new iPhone waking me up at 5:10 p.m. I took my time getting up from my little nap. There was no rush. I rolled out of bed awkwardly, grimacing from the pain of my recent emergency C-section.

I used the bathroom down the hall from the room I'd only slept in one night. I'd recently been moved to this hospital "family room" situated near the neonatal intensive care unit (NICU) where our new son, Elliot, was safely monitored by doctors and nurses. I'd spent the previous eight weeks in my own hospital room.

I fixed my hair and slowly made my way down to visit my five-day-old baby boy. Now that I had this nap in my system, I was ready to spend the rest of the evening by his side.

I stepped through the double doors into the dark and quiet NICU. I felt so proud to be mama to one of these little fighters. I dutifully headed to the sink to wash my hands with antibacterial soap. As I reached for the hand sanitizer, a nurse rushed up to me.

"They had to change Elliot's chest tube again."

I felt a flicker of annoyance and followed close behind her without finishing my ritual with the hand sanitizer. Approaching the window of Room #3, I found my baby surrounded by NICU staff. I felt nervous but also calm. This had happened earlier. He'd had a bit of a rough day because the chest tube keeping excess air from filling his chest cavity had failed. They'd replaced it, and he was stable after that. I sat at the nurse's station and watched the medical team through the glass window.

You see, God had made it abundantly clear to me that Elliot would live. He'd told me in a dream; he'd told me through prophetic utterances of friends and family; he'd told me through Scripture; he'd told me through Elliot's miraculous survival and through dozens of almost-death moments. God had promised Elliot's life. I believed my one job now was to believe God's promise. I had never in my life had such crystal-clear, unyielding faith—the kind that moves mountains and walks on water. My faith was a pure and polished mirror without one spot or speck. No doubts reached me, even as the NICU doctor came into the hallway and said, "It's not working."

Because of how purely I believed what I believed, nothing in the world could have prepared me for what came next. I walked into NICU Room #3, quickly writing on Facebook, "Pray now. The doctor thinks we are losing Elliot." But I knew we wouldn't lose him. I knew we'd see a miracle.

Ten minutes later, I held his lifeless body.

Naming the Unnamable

What is this book? I don't exactly know. I will talk about my faith, and certainly, this book is about my faith journey more than anything. But this is not a guidebook to faith practices or a lot of "we should, we never, we always" (I'll attempt not to preach, anyway).

This is not a book about infant loss. And yet it is.

This is not a book about grief. And yet it is.

This is not a book about trauma and post-traumatic stress disorder (PTSD). And yet it is.

This is not a book about religion, theology, or biblical interpretation. And yet it is exactly that.

It's not my autobiography, but in a way, it has to be.

After Elliot died that day, I realized I needed to write about my grief, trauma, and faith struggles in the now. To wait to write about how I felt in retrospect would not do the "now" justice. Only the me of one month after Elliot's death, or one year, or three years could tell the story of that day and moment and heartache accurately. So, I wrote. I vented on my laptop to a God I thought I hated. I wrote emails to a new friend, a mama whose baby had also recently died unexpectedly. I scribbled in my paper journals. And I became a blogger. I posted blog articles so others would know, would somehow understand, the dual nightmare of losing my child and my God in the same moment. I wrote to process my pain, grief, confusion, and gut-wrenching faith questions. I wrote so that another mama whose child was gone would maybe feel a little less alone. I share now so others experiencing spiritual trauma can find a companion on the journey and those who don't understand spiritual trauma might begin to understand.

After Elliot's death, I've looked back on that moment with an out-of-body clarity like watching an NFL slow-motion replay. I've wanted to run to that trusting, hopeful mother. I've longed to stop her, prepare her, embrace her, and weep to her, "I'm so, so sorry for what's about to happen." I can picture her, the me of June 3, 2017, walking into the NICU expecting anything but the death of her child.

In the wake of such unbelievable trauma and loss, I've had only my words to somehow find my way through the darkness.

So, I suppose if I could name what this book is, I'd say it is a wrestling match. It is a fight. It is a stubborn determination to not allow the darkness of death to overshadow my love for my son and my hope in Christ. This is the story of the battle for my heart, and, in a way, I believe it's the story of the battle for yours. In each chapter, I've included a blog article I posted during the first months and years of wrestling. These are not in chronological order, but rather a glimpse into various moments, denoted by stating how much time after (or in one case, before) that traumatic moment.

I wanted the miracle in my life to be my son's healing and his return from the brink of death, and I did not receive that. I wanted Elliot to live, to be my little boy who grew into a man. I wanted to change his diapers and help him potty train and take him to kindergarten and watch him lose teeth and become a gangly awkward teenager and take a thousand pictures at his high school graduation and let him walk me down the aisle at his wedding. I still want that. I will never stop wanting that. I have experienced a miracle, to be sure, but I would gladly trade in this miracle for the other. In a heartbeat.

But I can't. So, I receive with gratitude the miracle that I am slowly experiencing: I see light again. When the darkness closed in around me, nothing else existed. It seemed I'd live the rest of my earthly life not only without Elliot but also without the light of Jesus.

My reunion with Elliot will have to wait until this earthly life has ended, but my reunion with Jesus has begun.

This is a story of Christ coming alongside one broken-hearted mama, one furious and undone daughter, one religion-less wanderer. It is the story of him and me, and of all I thought I knew turning upside-down, so that now, perhaps for the first time, I'm seeing him more clearly through my messy, broken mosaic.

Who Is This Book For?

This book is for the faithful Christian who has only had the faintest whisper of doubts and does not see why I can't just trust that "the Lord giveth and the Lord taketh away." It is for the believer who has followed Christ in innocence and, like me, has found himself or herself lost in a darkness that comes after innocence is lost. It is for the searcher who really can't stand those conservative evangelicals but wants some sort of Jesus to believe in. It is for the conservative evangelicals. It is for the skeptic or the staunch unbeliever who wants nothing to do with religion, but when a loved one dies, wishes for a sliver of hope to see that beloved face again. It is for the wise follower of Jesus who is much farther than me on this journey, who can see me here still pounding the earth where my son is buried and is compassionately sitting by me in love.

I confess you will find in these pages some stoking of the fires of controversy. You will likely find my cynicism and blame seep through and aimed at unsuspecting recipients like Calvinist preachers and evangelical radio stations. It's not one person's "fault" that my faith in Christ was inexorably linked to my certainty-laced belief in God's sovereign control and promise of a miraculous outcome. I hope my journey will lead to a wide space of graciousness, where I don't assign undue blame to anyone. I'm working on that. There were many minor contributors over the years to a theology that was presented to me as "biblical truth," but was really a string of possible interpretations. I think we need to be more careful with that. We need to be careful not to speak for God, not to claim that we know what he says, how he means it, and what that means for the lives of others. It is not my intention to offend, but I think my own heart has enlarged with ideas I would have once found offensive.

Spiritual trauma is a real experience for myself and many others, and I have not seen this painful type of trauma often addressed by the larger Christian community. In my experience, the psychological and physiological effects of the shock of my son's death—the flashbacks, the triggers, the bodily reactions to memories—were aberrations to some of the believers who surrounded me. The fact that all the spiritual tools meant to comfort me—sermons, worship songs, the Bible—instead poured salt on the wounds in my heart caused confused Christians to smile politely and leave an awkward silence hanging in the air.

What exactly do I mean by spiritual trauma? If the dictionary definition of trauma is, "an injury or wound caused by an extrinsic agent," then spiritual trauma is an injury or wound to the living soul. This violent injury to my spirit is still a chronic ache years later. The fact that the extrinsic agent I've wrestled with has been God himself has left me and others who've endured spiritual trauma wondering how to sing Sunday morning worship songs or fill in the blanks in Bible studies. I know someone else out there is wrestling with our Creator this way; I hope I can walk alongside you, and perhaps we can wrestle together.

I hope, most of all, beyond my own heartache and pain, beyond my anger and cynicism, beyond the fall into black darkness from which there seemed no return, you will see the lines of light radiating through the cracks of my broken faith. It is Christ's light, and I am wondering if I've only just come to see it for real. He has always shown me light, out there in the stars, in here in my thoughts. His light broke through where and when I thought it simply was not possible.

And if he did that for me, he can do that for you, too.

Part One: The Mirror

Chapter One:
Among the Stars

I grew up in the country on five acres where the city lights of Denver could barely reach. On summer nights when I was little, my dad and I would lay on lawn chairs in the backyard and hold meetings of "Satellite Club." Satellites camouflaged themselves against the backdrop of a thousand pinpricks of light. I delighted in racing my dad to spot the satellites. I suppose this is when I fell in love with the stars.

When I was in high school, my parents bought me a telescope. Like with so many of my hobbies, I never became an expert at using it, and still don't know how to set the right ascension and declination. But I'd sit in our driveway and use the spotting scope to zero in on whatever caught my attention. I found Venus and Saturn, the Andromeda galaxy, and the moons of Jupiter. I also loved to pick out specific stars. I felt proud I could call out names of stars to friends: Deneb, Vega, Rigel…Follow the arc to Arcturus and speed on to Spica.

Spica. I remember well the night I focused in on that summer star. My amateur telescope didn't really make stars look much different—just bigger and brighter. But that night, when I homed in on Spica, something spiritual took hold of me. As I gazed through my telescope, Spica appeared so brilliant and blue and alone. It was an honest star, showing me how very brightly the divine burns in all creation. Using my story-making mind, I pictured myself there. I floated in the heavens with Spica, as far from planet earth as could be, hovering in the absolute stillness and quiet of space. I had the acute sense of realizing the same God who had made that star had made me, and he was as present within the fiery orb of Spica as he was with me at that moment. Because God was with me and with Spica, in a way, I was as present with Spica as I was in my gravel driveway. In God,

I was a different me—a me among the stars, cherished, transcendent of the struggles and strife of the earth, propelled to a greater purpose than I could keep in mind as an ordinary mortal.

Eventually, I had to come back to earth. I put my telescope away and went to bed. I probably had to bag groceries at my summer job the next day, which may have erased that mystical experience from my mind for the moment. But I never really forgot. The stars have called me back to moments of transcendence throughout my life, the same way the faces of children, the playfulness of dogs, the grandeur of mountains, or the pounding of the ocean have given me insights into reality. The presence of God is everywhere.

Many obstacles get in the way of seeing the whole of God's creation and my special place in it. I wish I could sit in Spica's orbit every moment, realizing just how beautiful my Creator is and how cherished a creation I am.

But life has a way of suffocating wonder. Those open, bright moments of transcendence with God can so easily be lost in the pursuit of college degrees and the frantic bustle of first jobs and apartments. Daydreams of falling in love captivated my imaginative attention. Grand visions of ministry filled the quiet spaces where God's whispers once dwelt.

And when pain came, the pain of being excluded, the pain of feeling unloved, the pain of living life without an irreplaceable person, two things happened. The pain at first was so loud, so all-encompassing, it seemed impossible it could ever quiet enough to hear a whisper of God's love again. But after the pain had screamed itself out, had gone hoarse from its defiant ramblings, only quiet remained. There was nothing anyone could say. Nothing anyone could do. In the aftermath of unimaginable pain, it was very surprising to find that God was still there. God is still love.

Blog Post: "Buried Under a Christmas Star"

Two years and seven months after

My girls and I spent several hours this weekend working on Christmas cookies to give to our new cul-de-sac neighbors. I confess it was fun the first hour or two, and then… *so. much. mess.* The flour everywhere.

The pans and bowls piled. The sprinkles. THE SPRINKLES!!! Let's just say I was a little more Grinch than Santa by the end.

But it was nice to awaken a tradition I began with the girls when they were just toddlers. The previous two years, we haven't done it. I remember a neighbor giving me some Christmas tins the Christmas season after Elliot died. "For your Christmas cookies this year," she stated. It was a nice gesture, but there were no Christmas cookies that year. It felt like a daily miracle just to keep my heart beating, and I felt nothing holly nor jolly about the season. It was a nightmare, to be honest, to try to pretend through a holiday designed to celebrate and spoil kids. I don't think I had yet emerged from the traumatic shock of the fact that my beautiful son's body was buried in a cold cemetery, rather than his hard-fought-for life filling our family with warm contentment.

The second Christmas after losing Elliot was easier, but it would be a stretch to say I enjoyed it. I tolerated it. We donated gifts to a little boy Elliot's age and saw how much it meant to his mother. My beautiful nephew, who is just eight months younger than Elliot would be, was with us for his first Christmas, and he also will always be a special recipient of the outpouring of my love for Elliot. But it still felt like a bad dream. The sweet excitement of the children all around me hammered into my heart: *someone's missing, someone's missing, someone is missing.*

And this year, my third Christmas without my Elliot, I was able to make Christmas cookies. It's a symbolic step toward joy in this season that is supposed to be joyful. Grief and trauma took the enjoyment of Christmas out of me, but I can feel a sparkle of it returning.

Jesus coming to earth as a baby has a deeper symbolism for me than it once did. God could've put on flesh any way he wanted; he could've made an already-grown guy like Adam. But he made himself a baby. This causes me to assume that the infant Jesus was not just prized and treasured because he was the Messiah. He was prized and treasured also because he was a baby. It was that little baby who caused the sky to gleam with heavenly host. It was that little baby whose star led foreigners on their adventure of worship. It was that little baby who had nothing but gave us everything.

If you are not in "the club" of infant loss, I am very glad. I hope you never will be. But after years in this club, hearing from moms and dads, embracing them in their tears, hearing the names of their babies, practically being able to see the broken hearts they wear each day, I am convinced we do not value these little ones as well as we should. We sing about baby Jesus and send Christmas cards with nativity scenes; we who love Christ claim this is what Christmas is about.

But parents who've lost babies remain wandering in a fog, uncertain how to continue remembering, celebrating, and including their babies who have died. Jesus died, yet we celebrate him as a baby every year. Would it not be a beautiful expression of our understanding of the value of baby Jesus to value all babies, especially heaven babies, in the same way? To say their names, place special stockings and ornaments in their honor, to love even more deeply in remembrance of them?

I love the symbolism of the "star" the wise men followed to locate the Child-King Jesus. We don't really know what that was, though I like all the theories. It doesn't seem we can see its light anymore. When Jesus came, he was declared the Light; perhaps the Christmas Star was an expression of his very being.

As Jesus was buried in the tomb, hope seemingly gone, we understand now that his Light was still shining. And, as one of my favorite verses from John states, "The Light shines in darkness, and the darkness did not comprehend it" (NASB 1995). Who could have imagined, let alone comprehended, the mystery of resurrection?

So, this Christmas, when the deep appreciation for the life and joy around me mingles with the ache for my missing pieces, I will remember. I will remember Jesus, too, died five days after a seeming world of possibility was just beginning. I will remember a mysterious star that led strangers to him as a young child. I will remember that his resurrection is meant to buoy my often-sinking hope. The same Light that woke him will awaken Elliot and awaken us all. It is the Light that causes my son's light to shine in Jesus' presence even now.

My little boy is buried, and there are days the weight of that fact crushes me. But this Christmas, I am intentionally remembering my son along with Mary's son and thinking of the Star's Light which connects them. I wish Elliot's precious hands were tearing into wrapping paper this year, and that his chubby cheeks were dimpled with joy at each new toy. I won't give in to forgetting; I will remember who he is, who he should be, and who he will be. Because he is not buried forever. He is buried under a Christmas Star, under the Light that overcame death and that forces my heart to have hope, if only a shred. I can't see this Star's Light the way the wise men could see it. But perhaps that makes it more real because "What is seen is temporary; what is unseen is eternal" (2 Corinthians 4:18 NIV). The light of this unseen Star guides me and places Elliot in my mind's eye as Christmas festivities unfold.

As the Father boldly declared his love for an infant in a manger two thousand years ago, he declares it for my Elliot this Christmas, and for me, and for all of us who are beloved children wrapped safely in his love.

Chapter Two: Cages

Waters of Baptism, Seeds of Doubt

I remember going to a sleepover at Mandi McCoubrey's house after I was baptized the summer between my freshman and sophomore years of high school. She and Lindy Frazier wanted to prank-call people. This had, previously, been one of my favorite pastimes, and usually, I was the instigator. It was only 1996, after all, and kids like me could dial numbers at random and say something embarrassing or profane without much fear of retribution. Caller ID and the *69 trick had gotten me in trouble a couple of times, but not enough to deter my bent toward obnoxious teenage behavior. If you ever had a pizza show up at your front door that you didn't order, that might have been me.

But just a couple weeks after being baptized, prank-calling felt like a big sin. After all, now that I was a real Christian, God was really watching. I think this was an early stirring of the Holy Spirit. I previously felt no guilt for disturbing a stranger's evening. Now, it bothered me. I didn't possess the inner security to tell my friends I thought it was a bad idea and why. Instead, I watched as they made their prank calls, and I laughed along reservedly, but I didn't participate.

They didn't invite me to any more sleepovers.

That was okay. I needed to be around "good" kids who wouldn't try to make me sin. At that time, I believed that my salvation was a precarious assurance, teetering on the edge of "walking away from the Lord." I always wondered exactly how many and which kinds of sins qualified as salvation-busters.

I grew up in a denomination called the Church of Christ. I don't blame the members of that church for leaving me with such a terrifying tightrope to walk. They believed a person is "saved" from hell (eternal conscious torment) only when that person is baptized (fully immersed as an adult or at least beyond the "age of accountability"). However, salvation was not some unchangeable forward progression, like a twentieth birthday forever leaving teenage years behind. It was more like a marriage contract, and I could be divorced if too many grievances added up. My eternal security depended on my continual obedience (*like, all the time??*) to ensure I would not lose my salvation. Not to mention the way I worshipped God: singing with no instruments, taking the Lord's Supper every Sunday, church three times per week, and only attending the Lord's one true New Testament church (ours, obviously).

The brothers and sisters in the Church of Christ believed this all, and to them, they were loving me by ensuring I believed the same. Can you imagine a believer fully convinced that baptism was the only path to be saved from an eternity of torment not encouraging others to be baptized? The theological constructs which had developed over hundreds of years for this group of believers were ingrained and absolute. They were doing the best they could with what they believed.

It was my first experience with the fact that the sincerity of a person's belief in no way makes his or her doctrine true by default. Conversely, it seems the more fiercely we clasp our fists around a particular theology, the more likely it's laced with assumptions and flaws.

It would be many years before I would question the theological points of my upbringing. For the rest of my high school years in rural Colorado, I just did my best not to commit any really big sins and say sorry very quickly for the little ones. I was prone to gossip and lust, jealousy and resentment, but it's not like I smoked cigarettes anymore. I thrived in my safe circles of friends, the theater and choir nerds, and felt a nostalgic sorrow when high school ended. All I had ever known was changing.

Being that a good Church of Christ girl goes to Church of Christ college, I chose Harding University way out in Searcy, Arkansas. The campus was pretty, and the bachelors were eligible. Where else would an almost-nineteen-year-old maid like me possibly find her first boyfriend and future husband all wrapped into one?

But college proved to be a letdown in the husband department, and I suddenly felt enclosed in a solitude that I was unaccustomed to. I was far from the family and friends I had been familiar with for eighteen and a half years. Even the trees of Arkansas suffocated me. I ached for the wide-open plains of Colorado, where gazing at the horizon gave my soul room to breathe.

I don't know if it was this first experience with depression, coupled with loneliness and the freshman fifteen (okay, twenty) that made me feel isolated from everyone, including God. I began to feel cynical about the whole thing—the Bible, the Church, my place in the world. My best friend from high school and I had been observing our friendship fizzle, much because of my Christian beliefs and her lack of any. She once said, "God creating people out of dirt? A big flood destroying the whole world? It just sounds like a fairytale, Heidi." I placed figurative hands over my ears to drown out her criticisms of my faith.

Of the Southern Cross and Instruments in Worship

During my sophomore year of college, I signed up to spend two summer months in Benin, West Africa, participating in a missionary internship. Four of us lived with missionaries and shadowed their work, learning what missionary life entailed. I left for Benin at the height of my first spiritual crisis of faith. It was an amazing cultural experience: learning some of the languages of Aja and French, learning the ways of life of people whose world was vastly different from mine, and trying goat meat from a communal pot offered by the chief's wife. The whole time I condemned myself as an inward fraud, barely believing the very truth missionaries taught. I displayed lighthearted smiles as I'd always done to keep people around me happy, without letting on how much I was struggling.

The missionaries treated us to a little weekend trip to the beach a few weeks into our stay. We splashed in the ocean and slept in a bungalow. We sat in the pitch-black night on the edge of where the sand met sea, and those stars God seemed to make just for me sprinkled light on my dark inner world. I remember the feel of the earth beneath me, imagining our little planet spinning and hurtling through the cosmos. I marveled that I was on another part of the globe so wholly different and far from everything I'd known. Even the stars were different. As I gazed south, the Southern Cross gazed back at me, and, again, if only I could have remained among those stars, I thought maybe things would be all right. It's amazing how much peace can persist when God's grandeur fills the sky.

But religion always seemed to reduce God to a handy pocket-Bible size. The conflicts I saw between my strict Church of Christ beliefs and what these Church of Christ missionaries were practicing increased the struggle. Once, we worshipped with a local congregation of believers on a Sunday, and I took out my camera. The missionary I was staying with said to me, "Just don't get the drums in the pictures." The people there were enthusiastically pounding out rhythms while voices joined in. It sounds so comical now, but I really didn't know what to do with the fact that I had always been taught that the Bible said not to use instruments in worship. Yet here these missionaries were participating in worship with drums and clearly trying to keep that fact from their American supporters. I see now that it was no crisis of belief for them. They had already let go of religious dogmatism in some respects to share Christ within a cultural context. It was still pushing in on me, though. I had, like many people, correlated my faith in God with faith in a certain set of interpretations and theological distinctives. I didn't know that's what I had done, and now I realize I was just barely emerging from childhood. Children see things in black and white by necessity; it's how they make sense of the world. No one had told me, though—because perhaps no one in my life was yet living it themselves—that all of life, and a journey with God especially, is replete with gray areas. More than that, life is filled with so many colors beyond black and white, it will take a lifetime for the eyes of our spirits to see them all.

So, there in my twenty-year-old head, I wrestled. One evening I tried reading my Bible and the words of my friend from high school raced around my brain, "It's just too much like a fairytale." I threw my Bible on the nightstand angrily, wondering if that was it. Maybe I had just lost my faith.

But the next day, the missionaries took us around the Beninwa countryside visiting local churches and pastors. I experienced a glitch in my brain. All these churches were not Churches of Christ! The missionary leading our expedition said something as we drove that might as well have been the theory of relativity for the wonder it brought forth in my imagination.

"When the people here see different churches and denominations fighting and arguing, they don't understand it. To them, they don't care what kind of church you go to. To them, there are just Christians."

B-b-b-but…my church had always taught me we were the one and only true church! And this man was telling me that just wasn't the way it was? I didn't have to stick to that hard-to-swallow narrative?

Before college, one evening in the late '90s, after we'd installed our first dial-up internet and bought our first computer, I thought about the "fact" that only baptized members of the Church of Christ would be in heaven. I searched (back then, we *Yahoo*-ed or "Asked Jeeves" more than we Googled) how many worldwide members of the Church of Christ existed on planet earth: a measly two million. Out of seven billion people. That's something like two-thousandths of a percent of the population. This unbelievable statistic gnawed at me, but I thought my maestros had the Bible interpreted just so, so I hushed my inner dissident.

I should've listened. Sometimes rebellion is very right.

Thankfully, Christ was there, never once condemning me for my naivete or blind faith. He met me in Benin, in the faces of beloved children of God so different than me, in the humbling hush of the starry nights. I think, though, I couldn't have digested more unlearning of untruth at that time. He brought me a gift of truth, and that was enough. That evening back in my hot hotel room, I read 1 John 2:2: "For He Himself is the propitiation for our sins; and not ours only, but of the whole world" (NASB 1995).

The. Whole. World.

Thank God it wasn't just my stuffy little club who'd be included in glory. I didn't realize it then, but this was the first taste of doubt turning to deeper intimacy with Christ (which, spoiler alert, would become a theme). Maybe it's why the doubts in the wake of trauma and the death of my child did not feel as forbidden as they seem to be for other brothers and sisters I've encountered. Doubt is the truest friend of faith I know.

How could it be otherwise? When my very essence as a mother

protecting my child got turned upside down, I was in such emotional pain I'd have welcomed physical pain instead. In this agonizing pain, you fight with God. Job did. You wrestle with God. Jacob did. You weep and shrug off God's consolation. Jeremiah did. You wish for death instead of a life of such agony. Jonah did.

Austin Fischer says in *Faith in the Shadows*, "Sometimes it is our faith that makes us feel we are losing our faith. A crisis of faith in the face of evil can be the truest expression of faith, because what we interpret as a loss of faith is often the growing pains of learning to live with a heart three sizes larger beating inside our chest. So, if evil (almost) makes us lose our faith, it might be because our faith is growing strong, not growing weak."

I didn't know I was growing a bigger heart as a young college student, and many college kids have epiphanies that change their faith journeys for better or for worse. I didn't know I had been wrestling with God as I doubted church doctrine. I didn't know what I didn't know. All I knew was that something was freed in me to see God as better and kinder than I'd been previously taught, and that excited me. I even tested out non-Church of Christ congregations by the end of college (gasp!). It felt like freedom, and I thought I'd been let out of a cage I'd never go back to.

But cages of religion just can't help themselves. We get free of one just to roost in another, and I was about to find myself caged again.

Blog Post: "Not Yet"

Two years and five months after

My youngest daughter turned five a few months ago. It's been almost two and a half years since she lost her little brother, Elliot—a brother she only saw as my pregnant belly and a cold, still baby in a casket at his funeral.

We've talked about heaven a lot since Elliot died. Really, having other children has increased the topic because kids have so many questions, and what good answer can we give them?

"Where is Elliot?"

Heaven.

"When will we see him again?"

Heaven.

"Why did God let Elliot die?"

Uhh...answer to be given in…

Heaven.

If the concept of heaven is abstract to the adult mind, how much more confusing it must be to children. Perhaps this explains the monumental fear that exploded from my Valerie a few months ago.

We were between houses and sleeping in one big room as a family in my parents' basement. Both girls were tucked snugly in their beds reading books, and I thought all was well. Sylvia, my older daughter, appeared and said, "Mom, Val is crying. I don't know why."

I went to Valerie's bedside and saw her clutching her blanket and crying real tears (not the kind when she just doesn't want to go to sleep).

"What's wrong, sweetie?" I asked.

Pause. Big explode. "I don't want to go live in heaven! I want to stay on this earth! I know I won't like it there!"

Talk about unexpected. We had not been discussing heaven anytime recently, that I could remember. But sweet Val has probably heard and participated in more discussions about it than many kids do their entire childhoods.

Valerie's outburst is not so different from how the idea of heaven struck me throughout my life. I felt comforted as a teen singing "Someday" around the church camp bonfire with my youth group, glad there was something after death instead of nothing. But it was never comforting in the sense that I wanted to *go* there. I think that's what Val was expressing. She has a brother with whom she was supposed to grow up, and instead we grown-ups tell her she'll only get to see him and know him in heaven. Oh, and that she will go there. She doesn't have a choice. Life leads to death. Thinking about all that can be heavy and scary, so I don't blame her for getting upset at the thought.

But something in me knows there is not such a sharp distinction between this and that reality, between life on earth and life in heaven, between now and then.

Sometimes, out of the corner of my eye, it's like I can see the truth: Christ in me has already placed me in heaven's realms. I'm not imagining things when I feel overwhelmed with the presence of my babies as if they are really here. Christ is with me, and they are with Christ. We are not apart; we are not living in two distinct realities.

I can't remember who first told me this interesting scientific fact, but it has been a confirmation for me of what I feel. Scientists have discovered in postmortem examinations of women that we mothers carry the DNA of our children in our brains for life. Male DNA has been found inside the brains of women who had sons. I found out Elliot's gender when I was just eleven weeks pregnant because of a blood test. They could tell from my blood that Elliot was a boy! The mingling of mother and child is not something I have cooked up for my own comfort. It is real.

But it must be even more real because not all women have babies, and men can't carry their children, and yet all of us probably have that person, whether it's a child or sibling or spouse or parent, who doesn't really feel "gone" after their death. It is not my intention to be mystical or supernatural about this, but truthfully, the existence of our souls after death is both of those things!

When I come to the Bible, the passages that speak to this reality are the ones that comfort me the most.

"...and raised us up with Him, and seated us with Him in the heavenly places in Christ Jesus" (Ephesians 2:6).

"For this perishable must put on the imperishable, and this mortal must put on immortality" (1 Corinthians 15:53).

"While we look not at the things which are seen, but at the things which are not seen; for the things which are seen are temporal, but the things which are not seen are eternal" (2 Corinthians 4:18).

I have been fixated on a poem called "Nondum" by Gerard Manley Hopkins lately. I've known the poem for years, but in the past few months, the words have resonated with me as if they were my own. To me, Hopkins articulates with startling accuracy the heaviness of this present reality in contrast to the transcendent beauty it contains. How can we have the stars of the night sky and also war? How can we have the crash of ocean waves and also children starving? And where is God in the beautiful mess of it all?

For some reason, in the fifteen or so years I've loved this poem, I never thought to investigate what the title, "Nondum," means. So, the other day, I looked it up.

It means "not yet."

It gave me chills to read that. If there are any two simple words that describe the way I feel many days, it would be those. Living in the "not yet" of this present reality while at the same time touching the fringes of the reality to come—there is something very deep about this I almost don't have words for.

"Not yet" is enjoying the breeze on my face while hearing something like a whisper from God.

"Not yet" is my heart delighting at the sound of my girls' laughing while my heart cracks because a little boy's voice isn't filling our house.

"Not yet" is my heart leaping when I anticipate adopting a child soon, while it also sinks to think of the millions of fatherless yet to be adopted.

"Not yet" is breathing in the beauty of the stars at night and breathing out a cry for justice to come to the billions suffering under those same stars.

"Not yet" is being surrounded by people I love and who love me and yet feeling like a stranger.

"Not yet" is knowing God and yet not having any clue about God.

"Not yet" is a desire to be wrapped up in the beautiful tangle of people we call the church while feeling completely awkward and out of place in church life.

"Not yet" is the well-worn comfort of old friends and the sad longing for how friendships once were.

"Not yet" is resting completely in Christ's love for me, and his love giving me the freedom to doubt, weep, laugh, and dance.

"Not yet" is a vibrant little girl crying that she doesn't want to go to heaven.

Hopkins writes in "Nondum:"[1]

> We guess, we clothe Thee, Unseen King,
> With attributes we deem are meet;

1 Gerard Manley Hopkins, "Nondum [Not Yet]."

Each in his own imagining
Sets up a shadow in They seat;
Yet know not how our gifts to bring,
Where seek Thee with unsandalled feet.

So much guessing. So much not knowing. It's not yet!

And still, there is present life to live. It's not enough to daydream about the far-off someday when in some literal or figurative fashion, Jesus will return and set all things right. There are days when the "not yet" makes me want to just lay in bed and wait for him so I can be with my little boy again. I wonder if "not yet" contributes to depression?

Paradoxically, "not yet" is what keeps the spark of hope glowing.

I just spent time in a conversation of the heart with a member of my extended family who has also lost a child. Her daughter, Jennifer, my little cousin once removed, died twenty-four years ago at the age of seven. When I think about it, that's the first death that ever grabbed my heart. I remember Jennifer was so beautiful, like a little porcelain doll. On our week-long visits to Iowa on summer breaks as a kid, I'd play with Jennifer and her siblings and catch fireflies in their yard. I remember a heavy sense of the wrongness of that little doll not being alive anymore, as much as I could understand and mourn her at the age of fourteen.

And now, speaking with her mom, being a mom myself of a child who lives in heaven, the sharing of understanding felt so welcome. She understood my longings and the mix of sorrow and joy at every moment. When we were finishing our conversation, she said, "Aren't we blessed to be their moms? Jennifer and Elliot's moms?"

Wow. What a significant statement. We are the mothers of these children. Present-tense mothers who are not yet with them, and these children in heaven have received the reality we are not yet able to live in. We're connected to heaven in a deep and abiding way.

Maybe the "not yet" of life is a blessing. It's the one hope that keeps despair from winning. There are times we can all look at the world and be overwhelmed by its wrongness. But the truth is: it's not yet done. It's not yet over.

"Beloved, now we are children of God, and it has not appeared as yet what we will be. We know that when He appears, we will be like Him, because we will see Him just as He is" (1 John 3:2, emphasis added).

Jennifer and Elliot and my aunts and uncles and grandparents and other friends and family who've gone before me: they see Jesus just as he is. And when he appears—oh! When he appears! I'll see my Jesus, and I'll see them too.

I guess that will help me keep going. What's the good of giving up? It's not easy, so along with Hopkins I make this request of God:

> Oh! Till Thou givest that sense beyond,
> To show Thee that thou art, and near,
> Let patience with her chastening wand
> Dispel the doubt and dry the tear;
> And lead me child-like by the hand,
> If still in darkness, not in fear.

Chapter Three:
Lookin' for Love y Propósito

All Part of God's (Secret) Plan

My certainty had shifted after college, but I was still so certain I could find security in some "right" understanding of it all. Since I discarded my childhood faith traditions, I began a subconscious journey for the *real* right church, theology, doctrine, and interpretation.

I found myself at a Vineyard church, which is about as far a cry from the Church of Christ as Hillary Clinton is from Donald Trump. I attended Lantern, a young adult ministry, and crushed on certain fellas, especially the ones that raised their hands while praying or singing. The people there were so...emotional about Jesus. Growing up in a church where worship was in the head, it was refreshing to learn I could incorporate my heart into loving Jesus.

I was neck-deep in the lives of a hundred sixth graders teaching at my first post-college job, middle school language arts. I was also the proud renter of my first apartment! I did not have a lot of money but had some time on my hands (as much as a first-year teacher can have), and I loved it. I spent hours in my little apartment with me, Jesus, and my mediocre guitar skills writing songs for the Lord. I sang my heart out and hoped my neighbors heard me. Those songs allowed all the emotion and love for Christ to pour out in an innocence mingled with pain.

I've always spent a lot of time in my head: pondering, wondering, creating poetry, feeling the weight of the world and the suffering of others. As an adolescent and college student, I kept these deeper inclinations on the inside, too self-conscious to share them with any but the most trusted confidants. Instead, I'd smile and goof around and keep the fragile parts of my heart safe from possible abuse or mockery.

But this new church experience helped me gain permission to

let the depth out, let myself know Jesus in a more intimate way and be vulnerable with others in the beautiful heaviness of what I was feeling. I even tentatively shared the songs I'd been writing with my big brother Ryan (a real musician). Over the next few years, he and I recorded dozens of my songs as he added all the music for the keyboard and other effects that made them sound pretty. We developed a sweet sibling bond through those recording sessions, and I was so enthusiastic about sharing my newly invigorated faith with him. Even now, when I listen to the songs that we recorded fifteen or more years ago, I am transported back to that time of innocence and trust. There was so much aliveness in it.

"Crown of Beauty"
I won't live deceived.
I'll drink truth, believe
That all You say is true.

I step out of time,
No hurry, no worry in my mind
And see your face so clearly.

Man of Sorrows, we looked away.
Our burdens you carried that day.
You had done no wrong.
But you willingly bore my shame.

What a thing to behold, what a mystery of love!
King of Creation, you wore this life, despised by men
You died.
What a truth to believe, what a victory is mine!
Death couldn't hold you, like the morning sun
Bright in my eyes
You rose.

As much as I enjoyed the fellowship with Jesus, I was lonely. I hoped daily for God's "plan" for my life to be revealed. I gleaned something new from the Vineyard and associated theology: God could talk to me, and not just through Bible verses. I was still learning how this mystical transaction took place. I started listening to Christian music (the irony of instruments being banned in "worship" meant I had never listened to Christian music before the age of twenty-four). I began a prayer journal, channeling all the writer's passion that had lived in me since I wrote "John and the Case of the Missing Computer" at nine years old. But now I was writing to God. And, strangely and wonderfully, in all the words that poured into my journal or the lyrics of another song, I really could hear him. I really could feel him. For the first time, I really could know him.

Young adulthood was an exciting journey, but I was also so insecure, like many twenty-somethings. I hovered between the worlds of childhood and adulthood. I repeatedly fell head-over-heels and wondered if this was the man God had "planned" for me (because apparently my future husband was like the Highlander and there could be only one!).

The fact that I keep using quotes around "plan" in relation to this idea of God's sovereignty over each detail of my life betrays my cynicism, of course. When I was in my early twenties, nothing was more comforting than to believe God had already figured it out. Whom I'd marry, where we'd live, what lives he wanted us to touch, the children we'd raise. The flight out of my childhood nest and into the scary skies of real life had made me feel utterly out of control. I needed to believe all details pertaining to my life were already written in his book, just waiting for me to act out the story in real-time as his beloved marionette.

And the teachings of my new church, the songs on my new favorite Christian radio station, and the commentary in my Beth Moore Bible studies said the same thing: God knows the future. God has a plan for your life. God will make sure that plan happens. You can hear God's voice. He will reveal his plan to you in time (though not directly; you'll have to follow heavenly breadcrumbs). Everything that happens in life has a purpose, and all events are in God's design and control.

It all sounds so simple. So utopian, even. And since I had not yet come face to face with my own personal trauma, I could accept my life thus far as perfectly designed by God. I could never have anticipated the underside of such ingrained theology. I could never have predicted how it would rip my heart right out of my chest with more force and pain and bloody brokenness than I had a framework for. I could not, in my bright-eyed wonder at such liberating ideas, have understood how I was beginning to build a shaky scaffold of faith in control and certainty. That rickety structure was, sadly, destined to come crashing down.

I didn't then know the theological terms I now hear more frequently: predestination, election, God's sovereignty, Calvinism. I didn't need it. God's plan for me was going to come to life; I just had to be obedient to him and look out for all the signs that were God's subtle and secret markers leading me in the right direction.

Well, would ya look at that—I have a crush on a guy I met on a mission trip to Juárez, Mexico. So that must be where God wants me next!

Falling In Love

Now, I shouldn't be too hard on my 25-year-old self. I did go on a mission trip to Juárez during my second year of teaching with no other motivation than to get out of my comfort zone and use my time as a single gal by telling the world about Jesus. I always loved other cultures, and the mission trip to Juárez was convenient and affordable. And while I was there, something in that city felt like home. "God's plan" aligning with my daydreams of romance gave me the nudge I needed to actually go. I signed up for a six-month internship with a mission organization. I put my teaching job on hold, packed as many of my belongings as I could into my Pontiac Grand Am, and drove south to Mexico.

This is a good example of how I now see God can use circumstances and choices. I was influenced to move to Juárez as much by my desires as by God; I can admit that now. But my decision to serve others, whether the design God had always planned for me or not, was able to be used by him. And use it he did.

I lived and taught English at a newly opened Christian elementary school in Juárez. It took me time to feel like I belonged (considering all the Spanish I knew was gleaned from a one-month immersion course in Guadalajara). And it took me time to find my bearings in relationships with the missionaries who ran the school, the children I was teaching, and their moms who were so darn polite I thought they didn't like me.

Within a few months, I had relationships with the missionaries, the kids, and the moms. And I had an even more dependent, trusting relationship with Jesus. I'd sit in my cinder-block apartment in the evenings belting out new songs for the Lord.

During my early days in Juárez, I thought I was there for more than just teaching English. I pictured myself pouring into the lives of adolescents at a nearby group home for teen girls. But all my attempts to minister to those girls ended in closed doors (literally), and I felt like quite the missionary failure. I went back to my little apartment dejected after my final attempt to spend time at the group home and wondered, "Well then, what is my purpose here?" Or, in all the Spanish immersed in my head, "¿Qué es mi propósito?"

And I felt the sweetest assurance from Jesus that even though the night hadn't gone how I had planned, it wasn't a waste. I wasn't spending the evening ministering to hurting teenage girls, but I was spending it with him. And at that moment, I'm sure I heard him tell me that there was no other place he wanted me. Even now, I can close my eyes and be transported back to that night when I wrote these lyrics:

> Do I bring a smile to your face?
> Do you know how I feel in your embrace?
> Shockingly lovely, your holiness rises
> Dancing and outshining the stars.
> Bow down the heavens, engulf me, my Jesus,
> This moment, this quiet is ours.
>
> Do I bring a smile to your face?
> Do you know how I feel in your embrace?
> Every knee will bow before you one day,
> Every tongue confess you are Lord.
> Here we are, talking late into the night.
> Ruler of the nations, I am precious in your sight.
> Call my name.
> Call my name.

I feel a pang in my heart as I type those words and remember that night. I fell hard in love in Juárez, though not with any fella. I grew to love the missionaries who ran that school and consider them family to this day. I fell in love with the students, their families, the Spanish language, and oh how I fell in love with Mexican sweet bread. But mostly, I fell more in love with Jesus, with the intimacy that came from depending on him for every second of my emotional survival. It was childlike faith, pure and innocent. I wonder if innocence like that is lost forever, or if it will be regained one day.

American theologian David Bentley Hart says, "Wisdom is the recovery of innocence at the far end of experience." I sure hope so. Some days, that kind of wisdom hovers over me, right where Elliot lives, and I know I'll be okay. On other days, I'm still too enmeshed in the experience of trauma and loss to feel anything else. For now, I will remember my 26-year-old self, sitting on a concrete floor in Juárez, Mexico when the world seemed to stop for Jesus and me.

Blog Post: "The Way Things Grow"

Two years and ten months after

We just returned from a brief trip to Juárez, México, to visit our dear friends, Maria and Gilbert, who run Anchor Children's Ministry. Besides just caring about seeing our friends, Dustin and I also wanted to visit since we are on the board and are deeply invested in what happens there. We want to pour our time, energy, and talents into helping the schools that are the main ministries of Anchor: Colegio Ganley (elementary) and Colegio Gamwell (junior high). But the last time we were there as a family was three years ago, right before I became pregnant with Elliot. We'd planned to go again as a family in March 2017 when we took a group from our church on a mission trip. But my pregnancy complications had become so severe that we knew it was best for me to stay home. Dustin led the trip without me, and while he was there serving, I called him with unthinkable news. Dustin remembers where he was standing and what he was doing when he got that call, and the idea of returning to Juárez had been impossible for him for the first couple of years due to the association with the traumatic moment that led to the death of our son.

But now, almost three years since that horrific day in which we received the painful news, Dustin was able to return. He still couldn't set foot in the building where he was when he received my phone call, but what bravery to return. While holing up in our cozy home and never getting outside our four walls might be easier, we must live what Elliot taught us, or we won't really be living.

The elementary school is in its 15th year of existence, and the junior high is in its third. I came to that place when the elementary school was in its second year and was still just beginning. The children I taught are now teenagers and adults, many with children of their own. I've seen amazing transformations in which families embrace Christ, embrace the challenges of breaking generational cycles, and embrace the hard work of being different. These lives have burst open with color against the gray backdrop of drug addiction and poverty. I have seen things grow in the thirteen years since I first encountered that remarkable place.

I have also seen kids and families I love stagnate into sameness, continuing generational cycles of broken families, drug use, perpetuating poverty, throwing away opportunities at education, and not allowing Christ to be real to them. It can feel discouraging. But I think I glimpse something I was not able to see so well before Elliot. If everything were judged just on how it appeared on the surface, we'd all have great reason to be discouraged. But Christ is a sustaining inner work, and I don't believe his work is ever done or that he's ever given up.

In the fall, I planted tulip bulbs at Elliot's grave. I don't know if I'm really supposed to do that, and I've had imaginary conversations with some groundskeeper trying to stop me as I get all wild-eyed mama bear and defend my right to take care of my baby's place however I want! Thankfully for all involved, no one has ever approached me in these tender and defensive moments. As I was planting them, the parallel became apparent between what I was doing and how it echoes what I'm desperately hoping for. These bulbs, dead though they are in appearance, have all the potential for colorful life just waiting inside them for the right time to bloom. My little boy's body is dead; this is a fact that never leaves me and stops breaking my heart. But could his body, that precious seed, still hold the same potential as a tulip bulb to break forth into colorful life one day? I don't know how resurrection works, if it's literally these same bodies or something on a higher plane that we can't comprehend, or perhaps both. But if the Creator created plants to die and be reborn annually, wouldn't he who counts us of much greater value than the lilies of the field have something beautiful in mind?

But it's not just an end-of-life someday hope, is it? Isn't that same marvelous germination toward abundance the life that Christ came to pour out? I think so. I think when things don't look promising on the outside, when things look as good as dead, we must maintain hope in Christ and his work in each human heart that there is the potential for a seed to take root and to grow into something colorful, fragrant, alive.

While I was in Juárez, I heard that one of my students from so many years ago is now in prison for transporting firearms. He will likely be there for a long time. It breaks my heart. I haven't seen him in over a decade, so all I remember is the toothy grin of a 9-year-old, one of those boys with too much energy that drove me crazy some days but usually kept me laughing. What happened to that innocent and lively little boy? What strongholds in his family history, lack of support at home, and poor decisions led him to that point? My first response to this news is to feel so let down, to think he is a lost cause, and to think it could have been different somewhere along the way, but now it's too late.

But that's not the way things grow.

Growth is less an instant appearance of completion and more a death that leads to transformation. Christ is there in that prison cell with my former student, in the cold silent grave that houses my baby, and in the slumbering seeds and bulbs awaiting spring's warmth. He is there.

I like to see things happen. I like to go to sleep at night, knowing everyone I love is accounted for, safe, and happy. But I've always known I cannot make this peaceable wish come true. I remember weeping many nights after I left Juárez, wondering what would become of the innocent children I came to love so dearly. What hope did they have when all the factors in their lives would constantly press against them to remain trapped in generational cycles? It seemed impossible and unfair. And then I became a bereaved parent, and I had to wonder: where is the hope in any of this? What is the point if it's all going to end in such pain, loss, and heartache?

I suppose if I could tell an acorn that it would one day turn into an oak tree if only it would allow itself to be buried and dormant, it would likely contest. It seems impossible. Yet God's teacher to us, nature, doesn't let us get away that easily. Impossible life from death happens every day all around us. Why should it be less true inside of us?

I think Jesus is fortifying my heart not to lose heart. It is so easy to lose heart. I lose heart when my daughter cries and needs to hold Elliot bear because she misses her brother so much. I lose heart when I see teen girls in Juárez pregnant before they're sixteen by guys who have no intention of being fathers to their children. I lose heart when a loved one feels that a healthy mental state free from crippling depression is impossible for him.

Christ Jesus reminds me that things are not as they seem. There is growth happening in the secret places, slowly, imperceptibly to us, and always in the view of him who made it all. I don't always see the way things grow in Jesus' economy, but they always do. Hope in this growth looks like waiting for a bud to bloom in someone's life, embracing small victories, and allowing the suffering in the world to create more compassion in me.

As the tulips and leaves bloom this spring, I'll see Christ's face in them. I'll let nature be his voice as he tells me again and again:

"Therefore, we do not lose heart."

"Por tanto, no nos desanimamos." 2 Cor. 4:16

This is the way things grow.

Chapter Four:
Babies and Bible Studies

My New Best Friend

The first time I saw Dustin, I was twenty-seven years old. I made my way up a flight of stairs to help a friend move out of her apartment. He was helping her too, and we both knew this was a setup.

He smiled as I arrived at the top of the stairs. *He is sooooo.... clean-cut*, I thought. I'd always had a bent toward the bad boy, and my previous love interest had had oodles of tattoos and piercings. Dustin had a nice shirt, nice haircut, and a nice smile. He seemed so nice. And thus, I didn't know if he was my type.

No one ever said girls make sense.

I had been back from my year in Juárez for about six months and was teaching at a local Christian middle and high school. I had become more content in my singleness, but thankfully, others were not so content and thus conspired to get Dustin and me in a room together.

By the end of that awkward day together, full of choppy nervous conversation, this nice guy found the courage to ask me to dinner. We went out the following Saturday, and after a couple dates, I realized something astounding.

I liked him. I really liked him. I mean, yes, I liked him in the sense that I was attracted to him, and I got butterflies in my tummy and holding hands made me all nervous and sweaty. But, more than that, I liked him in the way you like your very best friend.

And that, kids, is true love.

I vetted the guy, of course. I made sure he was open to adoption, which had already been on my heart for many years. I flew him down to Juárez with me for a quinceañera, to passively communicate: if you want me, you get Juárez. He easily passed all my silly tests because he really was the guy that I hoped he was. Kind and hard-working, conversational and deep. And he liked Star Trek, which took so much pressure off my nerdy mind. He felt like home.

We got engaged after nine months of dating and married six months after that. We were surrounded by friends and family and well wishes.

And I was so, so, so inwardly afraid we'd mess it up somehow. You know, the plan. *God's* plan. Was this really it for us? Is this really what *he* wanted? Dustin had been to Juárez with me on visits and mission trips, but he wasn't really interested in becoming a missionary. So, I kept teaching at a comfortable Christian school, Dustin kept working as an electrician, and we bought our first adorable little home. It all seemed too...easy.

Had I missed it? The plan?

I mean, I'd spent the last decade pining to get married, and now I was married, so why wasn't I more content? I thought we needed to be more spiritual, so I'd push Dustin to write in a journal and read marriage books with me. I hung verses all around our new house, trying to grasp "it," whatever it was. Something more real, some sense that I was still that special child of God writing songs in my room in Juárez. I felt like I was settling for a middle-class suburban life that was beneath me.

I poured myself into mentoring girls at the school where I taught and taking groups of teenagers on mission trips to Juárez. But I was getting restless. One day, while putting my hand on the belly of a coworker expecting her first child, it hit me. I felt that little girl wriggle inside her mama and a giant neon sign flickered in my brain: I. Want. A. Baby.

Parenting and Hell

Dustin and I had talked about having kids, of course, but we really wanted time to adjust to married life before that life-altering change. Now we'd been married two years, and I was ready. To my happy surprise, Dustin was ready too! The funny thing they don't really tell you is that you can't just snap your fingers and get a baby. It happens maddeningly easily for some couples. Not for everyone.

Once we really started "trying," it took about nine months to finally become pregnant. In retrospect, it was not long, but at the time, each month was a painful blow to my timeline and hope. And yet, we did get a positive pregnancy test, and the most miraculous thing of all was that pregnancy test turned into my first daughter, Sylvia. She was born in November 2012 when Dustin and I had been married three and a half years and were both soon to turn thirty-two. Sylvia was (and is) a calm sweetness pervading our home and lives. Her enormous blue eyes captivated us from day one.

Maybe being a little older when we became parents helped us feel confident to do things the way we wanted to do them. We were bouncing around between churches, trying to find the "one" before Sylvia came along. Then she came, and we just wanted to sit at home so I could nurse her and put her down for a nap whenever she needed. We listened to and watched sermons online for a while, and then my mom, the nicest lady you'll ever meet, asked if we wanted to listen to a sermon series about hell.

Uhhhh…..sure?

It was a set of sermons looking at hell from a perspective Dustin and I had never heard before. I resisted listening when my mom first approached me because the premise sounded too unbiblical. Too naïve. Wishful thinking, even. I mean, everyone knew that the Bible taught if you don't accept/believe in Jesus, you will go to hell, which is torment for all eternity. And there's no changing that after you die. For my mom to say this preacher down in Alamogordo, New Mexico had a different idea seemed arrogant, to say the least.

So, it was with a skeptic's scoff I began listening to Al Maxey expound upon the book *The Fire That Consumes* by Edward Fudge. Dustin and I would pause often and discuss; I'd scribble down notes because I knew I'd never remember all the scriptures and arguments for this position.

What occurred over several weeks and months of studying, listening, thinking, talking, and praying was that Dustin and I were convinced. We weren't convinced, necessarily, that all conclusions drawn by Al Maxey or Edward Fudge were complete. Their interpretations and opinions understandably seep through their wrestling with Scripture. But their ultimate point seemed to be supported by myriad Bible passages. They both settled on annihilationism as the ultimate fate of unbelievers, which became the stance that made the most sense to me. In a nutshell, without being within the eternal life of Jesus, we humans simply have no life after death. Life is found in Christ, so those not in Christ would experience "eternal destruction," as the Bible repeatedly phrases it. Eternal destruction, then, means to be annihilated, never to exist again. It made me wonder when and how the traditional view of hell had morphed into the "eternal conscious torment" churches so distinctly spell out in their statements of faith. The more I looked, the less I could find that common theology in the words of the Bible. I bet if you looked, you'd be surprised (and maybe relieved?) to find it's not there.

I don't know if Dustin and I were so much converted to a new theology of hell as we were released from the duty of believing in the old theology of hell. Once Al Maxey and Edward Fudge pointed out some obvious flaws in the eternal conscious torment theory, it was like a house of cards came tumbling down. And I was so glad.

It felt like a release similar to being let out of my cage of Church-of-Christ-only theology in my twenties. Once again, I was given the gift by God to see that just because the upper echelons of my faith tradition *said* something was true didn't *make* it true. It didn't make the opposite true by default either, but each release from a prior inaccurate view of God helped me draw nearer to him. I felt like Nicodemus slipping secretly away from his Pharisee cage of convention, finding Light in the cover of night.

I had always had a nagging irritation with the idea of eternal torment in hell for unbelievers. It seemed so…extreme, so unfair. I remember thinking but never voicing, "If Jesus supposedly took our punishment, why would people go to hell? His punishment was getting beaten and hung on a cross and suffering for several hours, sure. That was awful. But it doesn't even come close to suffering forever. If Jesus were really to take our punishment, then he should be in eternally conscious tormenting hell." Add to that the conundrum of why God would create humans in the first place if the vast majority would be tortured forever. "God is love" doesn't quite ring true in light of such a thought. Indeed, I wondered why any of us Christians would even dare to have children if there was even the smallest chance our beautiful little ones would be "unbelievers" who'd burn for eternity.

Strange that I never felt safe sharing such deep-seated and valid objections. Shouldn't we feel free among brothers and sisters on this same journey to do exactly that? And yet it felt the powers that be would not have listened. But with each new insight into the fact that God and God alone could guide me out of religion and into truth, I was gathering more confidence to question human doctrine. I did not have to be put in my place by a hierarchy of religious "experts." I answered and still answer to a higher call, a higher love, a higher purpose. Once upon a time, "correct" doctrine taught the sun moved around the earth, which we all accept as an erroneous view now, despite verses in the Bible that seemed to indicate that very idea. Why is it so hard to believe our current theologies and doctrines might not be infused with similarly inaccurate assumptions?

Dustin and I finished that sermon series markedly changed in our view of one small (but important) area of doctrine. We no longer adhered to the traditional view of hell, and I felt such a deeper closeness with my heavenly Father. I rejoiced that the intuition in my spirit, which resisted this doctrine for many years, was valid. God was not some cosmic torturer, creating billions he knew would be tormented forever. The Jesus with whom I wrote songs in my cinder-block apartment in Juárez, the one who met me as a teenager hovering in Spica's orbit, the one who told me I was cherished just because he loved me, not for anything I did or didn't do, this same Jesus loved everyone that way. And now I didn't have to try to swallow a bitter pill of a doctrine that seemed inconsistent with his love.

Changes

In July 2014, nineteen months after Sylvia was born, we welcomed our second daughter, Valerie. She came bursting in the world like a firecracker, impatiently deciding to be born at home in the presence of firefighters rather than at the hospital with a doctor. I love my unconventional girl.

Being a stay-at-home mother (SAHM, for those who like acronyms) afforded me time to develop new friendships and spend one-on-one time with people while my fabulous mom did some babysitting. I joined intensive Bible study groups, then added on a couple of one-on-one Bible studies with people in my life I thought could benefit from my guidance.

Little aspects of my faith journey had shifted up to this point in my life, and I thought they were big changes, but in retrospect, they really weren't. They were like changing my shirt, whereas what was to come was like replacing my entire body with new parts. And I'm still in that process of transformation. This kind of transformation is more laborious and painful. Putting on a new idea about hell or how to take communion can help keep faith fresh and alive. New ideas can also cause new arrogance (the "I'm right; you're wrong" syndrome), and I am just as susceptible as anyone to that flaw.

But I was in a good place in my mid-thirties, two babies, and so much aliveness in my spirit. I'd sit on my chaise lounge while my girls napped and work through all my Bible study books, write in my prayer journal, and keep the fire alive in my heart. We even landed at a new church that seemed about perfect: small, down-to-earth, "biblical." I don't think I was proud, as if I'd arrived. The opposite, almost. I was very thankful, very content. I knew life did not promise to be easy. But I knew God promised to be good, and I thought I knew what that meant.

Blog Post: "Two Versions of Me"

One year and four months after

One of my favorite features of the Denver International Airport is the long, long moving walkway. I like how it helps travelers traverse the great distance across terminals at exponential speed. It's gratifying to step on an already-moving conveyor belt and become strangely quick with minimal effort. Passing by all the regular pedestrians on the stationary floor gives a sense of gliding along like a gazelle.

I don't know if *way* back in the late nineties (just stop reading if you weren't even born), you happened to see a little Gwyneth Paltrow film called *Sliding Doors*. At the beginning of the movie, the Paltrow character misses her subway train (or does she?), and for the rest of the film, the viewer is given insight into two versions of Paltrow, two alternate realities of her life: one if she had made the train, and one if she had missed it.

Sometimes it feels like there are two versions of me, two realities that must exist because there's no other option. I can't erase either version because both now define who I am.

One version of me is on the moving walkway because that moving walkway is time. It's impossible to stop. I couldn't get off it if I tried. My husband is there, and my kids are there. The daily requirements of cooking, cleaning, wiping snotty noses, and eating chocolate are there.

The other version of me stands on the stationary ground next to the walkway. I am watching my other version be carried away by the necessities of time and living. The stationary version of me holds Elliot tightly to my chest, cradling his memory as any mommy cradles her baby. I also watch friends and family moving along the walkway, as new babies are born, houses are sold and bought, children grow up, and holidays and birthdays come and go with every season.

One version of me had to get back on that moving walkway. Occasionally, I've heard people observe that a bereaved person seemed to be "moving on," as if it's a sign of healing willpower. Well, I can't speak for other bereaved parents, but I know for me, that is not the case. As much as I wanted to stop time when my son died, I had no power to do so. I am alive in this world, and time is relentless. "Moving on" is just the reality that I can't stop the walkway. How can it be fall once again? Soon it will be Christmas and another new year. And the me holding my little baby boy seems to fade further into the background.

And yet I am still her, still also the version who will never, who can never, "move on." I am gazing at the face of the baby this body bore, whose birth scar I forever wear. I am holding the hand of a little boy who wrapped his fingers tightly around mine, whose perfect clear eyes I gazed into. I am in awe of my son, who fought so hard for his brief life. I smile at the thought of a little boy who almost died during delivery but who would never give up. I remember how he cupped his hands to his face, and the delicacy of his legs as I changed his diaper. I am her. I am that mommy. Elliot's mommy. This is the version of me who can't fathom changing my Facebook profile picture or removing his framed photos in my home.

These two versions need each other. They poignantly intersect and keep teaching one another how to live and love.

The version of me who moves along the walkway of life, who navigates the daily rituals of home life and who makes up silly songs and dances to Latino music, owes so much to that lady on the sidelines. I look back at her, still holding Elliot, and am reminded again and again and again…I am on this conveyor for now. There is an ending, which will really be a new beginning. Someday I'll get to the end of the line and take a step off into forever.

One book which has kept me sane since losing Elliot is *Imagine Heaven* by John Burke. At first, I was skeptical because the whole premise of the book revolves around near-death experiences. But once I read it, I was convinced that people really have experienced foretastes of what awaits us in eternity. Reading those testimonies reminded me of Paul and John in the New Testament disclosing their glimpses into the mystery. One of the pictures the book paints that encouraged me most was the way people there experienced (or didn't experience) time. Jesus' realm is a timeless place, where these observers neither felt rushed nor slowed. They could experience each precious moment for as long as they liked.

What will it be like for time to stop its relentless progression at the very moment I get to be reunited with my son? Will I hold him for eons before I let him go? Maybe. That mental image reminds me of the version of me standing on stationary ground, holding onto my Elliot. It's the me who truly is a "stranger and pilgrim in this land."

But the version of me on the walkway must keep moving. Time gives me no choice. So, I watch the girls grow and lose teeth and become adept at monkey bars. I have lunch with friends and meet at parks for playdates. And the me on the sidelines gains strength from the version of me who keeps moving, knowing that she honors Elliot's memory as she gives to and loves her other children.

Usually, the two versions of me take turns. Unlike the first six months or so after losing Elliot, in which I now recognize I was probably trapped in the initial shock of PTSD, I have some control over how I deal with triggers when they appear. I must live most of my life on the walkway. And if there is a trigger, like seeing a baby around Elliot's age or hearing a sound that reminds me of being in the hospital, I can take a deep breath and tell my grief and trauma I will deal with them later. Then, when I am alone or maybe in conversation with a trusted friend, I will allow myself the freedom of being the mommy on the sidelines, holding my Elliot and mourning him all over again. And when all the inner depths of my broken heart have once again had a chance to weep until no tears remain, I step back on the moving treadmill of time.

The hardest moments come when I'm in a situation where both versions of me need to have expression, but they cannot. When I really need to focus and parent my children, or in a situation where it would be socially awkward to let my tears freely fall, the two versions spin round and round in my head. In these moments, PTSD seems to be stronger than all my willpower or rationality. In these moments, panic sets in and nothing makes sense.

Be patient with people in your life who've experienced trauma. They truly cannot help how they might react when the two versions of themselves collide.

The difference, I think, between a traumatic event that is purely negative and one that surrounds the life and death of a loved one, is that "letting go" of a purely negative trauma can give the trauma victim a lot of freedom. For those of us who've lost loved ones, and especially who've lost children, we can't let go. I can't let go of everything that hurts about Elliot's death, because all of it is inexorably linked to Elliot's life. It would not give me freedom to erase the version of me on the sidelines. It would be a painful prison, locked into a silence where I didn't feel free to share about my son.

So, I share about him. I weep that I am missing out on a whole lifetime with him. I rejoice that I will be spoiled with an eternity with him. I choose to be with him once again. And there, in the slowed-down timeless place, I find courage and strength I couldn't find anywhere else. This is just another gift my son gives to me: the gift of being able to step off the treadmill of time, remember what once was, and fix my eyes on what will forever be.

Chapter Five:
Blood and Sorrow

Avery Rose

I wondered if we'd get pregnant easily again or not. It seems so naïve now, foolish even, that I didn't consider a third possibility. Either we'll get pregnant and have another baby, or we won't get pregnant, and that's how we'll know it's time to adopt. Every mama who's ever carried and wanted her baby also carries an underlying fear that her baby might not stay safe and growing in her womb. But before loss happens, and when your history says your body can easily make and carry babies, there really seems no reason to fear.

I proudly announced to my family on Christmas that we were pregnant by giving my brother a goofy card from his future niece or nephew. I still have the video of the reveal of that baby's life. It was early but, again, I had no reason to fear.

My first eight weeks of pregnancy passed without a blip. At my eight-week appointment, I saw a sweet little form on the ultrasound screen and heard the beautiful music of a steady heartbeat. I took the fuzzy black and white pictures home to show Dustin and the girls the first photo of the next member of our family.

Martin Luther King Jr. Day that year, January 18, I was nine weeks pregnant. My parents had taken the girls for a sleepover. Dustin was off work, around the house somewhere, completing home improvement projects. I would be tutoring in a couple hours but wanted to get a quick workout in first. I'd exercised through both pregnancies with my girls and believed it was a healthy way to take care of myself and baby. I finished thirty minutes on the elliptical then used the restroom.

Blood.

Not much. But blood in pregnancy. Heart-stopping, scary,

unknown. I'd had tiny scares of bleeding in both previous pregnancies, so I swallowed deep and didn't panic. I talked to Dustin; he reiterated that I should not panic. This had happened in the other pregnancies. Everything was just fine.

So, I decided to go to my tutoring session. I just thought I'd get through it, then call the doctor. I was teaching three teenagers Spanish verb conjugation and stood up to write on the whiteboard.

Horror.

Warm liquid soaked me, saturating my jeans down to my ankles. I hobbled to the bathroom, bright red blood everywhere. A parent of one of the students took me home. Dustin rushed me to the doctor. There was blood all over the seat of the car. I remember wondering if my jeans would be ruined.

My favorite nurse practitioner, Pam, met us in the exam room. She got the ultrasound machine ready. I knew what she was going to say. I knew it must be a miscarriage.

"Oh, there's the baby."

What? My baby was still there? My baby's heart was still beating? How had I lost so much blood and my precious baby was still living inside me? I didn't know something like this was possible!

The emotions of that moment. The overwhelming flood of joy and relief. God had brought us a miracle; a real, no-other-explanation miracle. Pam explained I'd experienced a subchorionic hemorrhage, and that most women go on to have normal pregnancies. She gave me a printout and we were on our way, flying so high with relief I thought we'd float away. We went out to eat and to see a movie. We thought we lost our sweet baby, and we didn't. Our third child was still safely growing inside my womb.

I woke up at about three a.m. with a name lingering in my mind: Avery. I remember since I didn't know if the baby I carried was a boy or girl, it could be appropriate either way. I fell asleep again, so grateful the nightmare from the day before was over.

As I stepped out of bed the next morning and walked toward the bathroom, a clot of blood fell out of me and onto the carpet. *It's okay.* Pam told me I might have more bleeding. I cleaned it up, shaking and nervous, but holding on to what I thought was a miracle from God. I sat at the dining table and tried to eat Frosted Mini-Wheats when suddenly I felt warmth saturate my pad, panties, and pants. I rushed to the bathroom where it seemed like all my insides began falling out into the toilet. Horrified, I scooped everything out of the toilet with my bare hands and put it all in a red Solo cup. *If this is what I think it is, I can't let my baby go down the toilet.* I sat in the empty bathtub as the hemorrhaging continued and called Dustin. He came as soon as he could and took me to the emergency room.

As I lay in that cold, sterile room, I begged God for another miracle like the one he'd given us the day before. *Please, please let this baby still be there. Please, please, let this baby live.* The ultrasound tech callously inserted the ultrasound wand. She didn't say anything for what seemed like way too long. I finally asked, "Do you see anything?"

"No," she replied. "I'm sorry."

A whirlwind of sorrow overtook me at that moment. How could my precious baby have been inside me less than twenty-four hours earlier, heart beating and her body squirming on the ultrasound screen, and now she just wasn't?

The first thing I told Dustin through my tears was, "I want to name her Avery Rose!" He, of course, said we could. We drove home, and I felt guilty for eating part of his sandwich on the way. How could I be hungry when my baby had just died?

I picked up that red Solo cup in the bathroom and carefully held the contents in my hands. There, in a little sac still intact, I saw my Avery Rose. I could see her head formed, little spots that would become her eyes. I was terrified of handling her too much, so I wrapped her up. I didn't take any pictures. I didn't look at her again. I wish I would have.

I slept with her next to me that night and held her through the morning. Dustin built a coffin. Then we drove to my parents' house and buried her, along with an irreplaceable piece of my heart.

What does a mama do with this? Even today, as I let myself return to that memory, every cell in my body cries out to change reality so that never happened. I see a little girl running alongside her sisters. She's got darker hair than Sylvia and a big smile. She's Valerie's playmate. Sylvia reads her stories. This is the life it should've been with her.

Looking back, it's shocking how I just accepted the loss of this precious baby as "God's will." I've kept journals for all my children, starting to write in them as soon as I found out I was pregnant with them. I wrote in Avery's journal, *For some reason, God's purpose is fulfilled by you being home with him now. I would still take you back in a moment, but I can see how even in my grief, he is working on me through your loss.*

I just didn't question if my miscarriage of Avery Rose could have been anything other than God's plan and purpose for my life. It was such an absolute. I had to find a way to push my pain through the pinhole of that belief. I don't really think it comforted me. I said the words and wrote the words because I'd been conditioned that that's just what good Christians do with suffering.

Six months after losing Avery, I was still missing her so badly. I remember pulling into my garage one day after grocery shopping and crying out to God that it wasn't fair. I ached for her. I closed my eyes and pictured the following storyline. It played out before me like a movie. I look back and see that as a moment of grace, and I didn't know just how much.

"Avery's Birth Story"

Six months after Avery, Eleven months before Elliot

She opened her eyes to a sparkling rainbow, which surrounded a throne. The shimmering colors took her breath away, and her first smile broke out upon her carefully created face. She'd never seen before, never breathed, never smiled, and yet all these things came to her naturally, like rain falling without ever learning how. She fixed her eyes on the One seated on the throne. No one needed to tell her this was the King. After all, he was her maker, her Savior, her friend.

"Welcome home, Avery Rose," were the first words, the first sounds her heavenly ears ever heard. His voice was as big as thunder, yet gentle as a breeze. The King stood and walked to her, drawing her up in arms so big they also held all of Creation. This was her very first touch, her first embrace. She buried her face in his robe, laughing at the joy of being alive and being completely home.

The King set her down gently and studied her. "My, what a

beautiful child of mine you are!"

If our eyes could've seen her, we may not have known whether to call her an infant, for she certainly was as new as a newborn; a child, for she was small and filled with wonder; or one already grown, for she knew and was known as much as any aged person. She was heaven-made, one of the precious children of God who were born straight into his presence. Her body bore none of the signs of mortality, only immortal light. Stars longed to shine as brightly as she.

Avery knew she was a child of the King. And yet, there was someone else, somewhere else. She looked to the King to fill in the knowledge she had not been given yet. Her heart told her that for the rest of eternity, she was to come to the King to be her answer. Her blue eyes lit up with the fun of it all! She readied herself to use her words for the first time.

"I'm home, King, but is someone missing?" Her words danced on heaven's air like a melody. She was sure she glimpsed an angel or two fly by, smiling.

The King knelt down to her level. "Let me show you something, Avery." He lifted his hand to touch a locket she just now noticed hung around her neck, resting gently on her white dress. King Jesus lifted the locket and opened it. A woman's face smiled from a portrait inside.

Avery's face lit up as she squealed, "That's my mommy!"

The King chuckled and put his arm around her. "That's right!"

Avery paused for a moment, unsure. The King reassured her. "You may ask me anything, my child. There's a reason I created you without knowing all things. I love to answer your questions."

She stared at the picture for a moment, then into the deep ocean of Jesus' brown eyes. "Well, my mommy has such a pretty smile, but her eyes look sad. Why?"

King Jesus nodded knowingly. "The smile is on her face because she knows she is mine. The sadness is in her eyes because her arms ache to hold you. Your mommy lives in a foreign land, and she misses you."

Avery looked again at her mommy. She knew her well. She'd spent a little time in that foreign land with her, inside her mommy's womb. For seven weeks in mortality, she'd heard her mommy's heartbeat, her breathing, her voice. She remembered her mommy singing, and almost thought she could hear her singing now.

She cocked her head to one side. "Doesn't my mommy know she'll be coming home soon, too?"

King Jesus lifted her up to hold her and began walking with her in his arms as they talked. They drew to the side of a stream where the banks were covered with green grass and flowers. Other children ran and played and beamed at King Jesus when they saw him pass by. As they walked, Jesus answered her.

"Your mommy, along with all my children who are in the foreign land, know they will come home one day, yes. But it is a hard wait for them. They don't know the grace of eternity yet. While they live in mortality, each day is a struggle. But the eternity I've placed in their hearts will carry them until they are home."

The concept of waiting was difficult for Avery to comprehend. Here, in Jesus' arms, there was only joy and wonder and fun. It wouldn't be a wait at all for her; just an eager anticipation of being held by her mommy.

The gold locket in her hand sparkled and Avery had another thought. "There are more, aren't there, King?"

The King bounced her in his arms and laughed. "Well since you mentioned it, there are many more!" And at that, the locket presented her with the picture of another face she knew well.

"My daddy!" she cried. Oh, she loved him. Her daddy was so strong but so gentle. She could already picture taking walks with him along this very stream when he came home to be with her.

Then the locket became a stream of pictures: her sisters, her grandparents, her aunts and uncles, friends who knew her name…the anticipation of having them here with her grew. What fun they would all have, what adventures with Jesus, what special stories their lives would create!

"Thank you for my locket, King. I will like looking at my mommy's smile and my daddy's kind eyes while I wait for them to come home. It will not be long."

Jesus sat down on the bank of the stream and set her next to him. He picked a flower and placed it in her hair. "No, dear one, for you and me, it will not be long at all."

Avery's brow furrowed again. Another question was forming, yet she didn't know quite how to put it. "King Jesus, how…I mean why…I guess…what was…?"

The King tousled her blonde hair. "I'll help you with this one. You're wondering why didn't you live in mortality, in that foreign land with your mommy? Why did you come straight home?"

Avery nodded, eyes wide in wonder. Jesus laughed and answered, "Well, I have a plan and purpose for all my children, a plan that touches lives and shapes eternity. But there is also an evil one who wants to shake my plans. He can shake these plans, but he can never truly break them. So, although you leaving your mommy so soon was not a good thing, I am the Redeemer. All the goodness I have intended for you, your mommy, all my children, I will redeem it all in time, and then the enemy will never shake my plans again."

Jesus' eyes seemed to grow warmer, if that was possible, with a new word that came to Avery's mind: compassion. He continued: "One of my redeeming gifts to your mommy is the way your early departure from the foreign land has touched many lives."

"Even though it makes my mommy sad?"

Jesus smiled and nodded. "Even though it makes your mommy sad. Even in her sadness, she's found a deeper hope, a deeper longing for her home in heaven. It's one way I will protect her heart through the sadness of the foreign land. Because of you, Avery Rose, heaven has become more real for her."

Avery thought she understood. She looked around at the other little children who played by the stream. She noticed they all wore lockets, too. Her heart beat fast at the thought of all the mommies who would soon be coming home from the foreign land. She pictured their faces, with beaming smiles and eyes that were no longer sad, running to embrace their little ones.

Avery leaned her head against King Jesus' chest. "I do miss my mommy, but I'm glad I'm home. I can't imagine being any place else."

They stayed there a while in contented silence. Children all around them laughed and played, while the presence of their King gave them life.

Everett James

It was a sweet story, and I'm still glad I had the comfort of it. Some days, my mind lingers on it, hoping it really was a vision from Jesus of where my babies are and how well they are loved. But a few weeks after writing this story, when I found myself pregnant again, then bleeding again, then losing a second sweet baby just twelve days after finding out I was pregnant, I started recoiling at some of the things I'd written.

"I have a plan and purpose for all my children," I'd written as what Jesus had spoken to Avery Rose.

I wrote in my journal just hours before going to the doctor while the lifeblood of Everett was falling out of me, *Why God? Why couldn't he have been a part of our family? I so wanted to hold him in my arms, touch his soft skin, kiss his little cheeks. I wanted my baby, and my heart is broken. Again. I wish there could be a miracle. Did my baby die because I didn't have enough faith?*

Here I was, holding another tiny dead baby in the palm of my hand. I named him Everett James. This time it was lonelier. No one knew we were pregnant. Dustin did not seem to mourn him as I did. I slept in the spare bedroom with Everett next to me for a week. I didn't want to let him go. He was supposed to be my "rainbow baby," redeeming the awful nightmare of losing Avery. We took him to my parents' home again to bury him next to Avery. No one else came. It was dark outside and dark inside me. Something was starting to unravel, but I couldn't put my finger on what.

My journal's words reflect the threads of beliefs that I was desperately trying to keep tied together but were inevitably on their way to unraveling.

How can I see my existence as part of your bigger, better plan?

Could I release every condition I have in mind that dictates how, when and why more children enter our family?

Can I rest in you and your plan?

Even if your plan means more miscarriage?

Even if your plan means failed adoption?

Even if your plan means no more children?

Even if your plan means far more children than I would plan?

Even if your plan includes pain, death, or loss?

Why did I live in such certainty that it all had to be "God's plan?" It frustrates me now. It hurts me for the woman whose life was hurtling toward such a height of hope to end in such a violation of that hope. I equated God's love with God's control, a fatal flaw for what was to come.

Blog Post: "My Glass Heart"

Two years and two months after

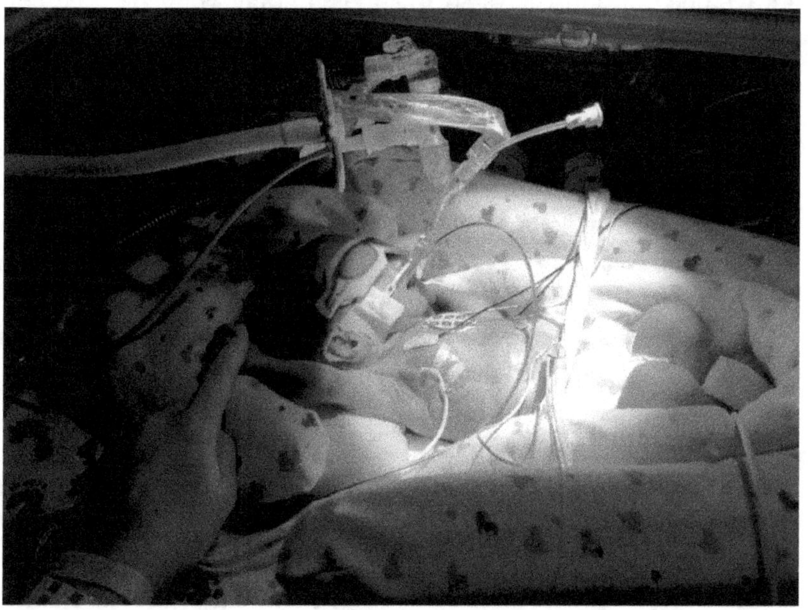

I took this picture twenty-six months ago yesterday as my precious son held onto my finger. Twenty-six months ago today, this perfect little love died in my arms.

The first year after Elliot died was a blur of days spent weeping, mourning, remembering, and memorializing.

The second year was an abrupt desperation to *do* something. So, we fostered our little C, and it was precious and hard and had so many nooks and crannies of emotions I still don't know how to process it fully.

This third year has been busy so far. We moved. I got a new job.

We're starting the adoption process. I'm gearing up for a homeschool year.

I don't cry most days. I can usually talk about Elliot without a quiver in my voice. I can glance at his pictures without emotion. Or I look away before the emotions have a chance to turn into that lump in my throat or that burning in my eyes. I look away because I can't bear to feel it anymore.

It's buried deeper now, my broken mama's heart. It hasn't healed, hasn't become some inspirational testimony to growth after adversity. It's wrapped up most days so I can keep going with life. The new house, the new job, my sweet girls—they are the wrapping to cushion my glass heart and keep it tucked away.

I think this is necessary. When I think about what's inside my broken mama's heart, I know I could not function through this life with the reality of Elliot's death constantly at the forefront of my mind. It sounds melodramatic, but if I remained in the space that I occupied the year after he died, I think I would eventually die of a broken heart.

So, my broken heart has had to descend to an inner part of me I don't access all the time. I'm realizing it's not denial; it's protection. And I don't think I am the one protecting it.

I think Christ is there, inside of me, a sentry guarding my glass heart. He doesn't think it needs to be fixed. He thinks it needs to be cherished, protected, and loved.

We unwrap it sometimes, Jesus and me, and we cry and cry and cry. We're unwrapping it right now, smiling at the days Elliot kicked inside me and burst into this world and held my finger, and blinked his eyes at me. We're laughing together at how stinkin' cute he was. We're crying together, Jesus and me, and pounding our fists at the unfairness of a little baby boy dying needlessly and cursing the suffering that daily afflicts our world. And we're gazing to the horizon, waiting for a day to dawn when suffering and death blow away like ash.

Jesus agrees with me: "This pain is excruciating. But this love is so beautiful." And he kisses my glass heart and wraps it carefully up in layers of life and work and sunsets and friends and laughter and chocolate sundaes. He keeps it hidden on days he knows I can't bear it. He says, "You don't have to look at it today. It doesn't mean you love Elliot any less." He knows many days I can't talk to him because prayer feels like grief. So, he wraps arms of unrelenting acceptance around me and reminds me, "You're not performing for anyone. You already have my love."

So tomorrow I'll wake up and drink some coffee and make it through another day, knowing deep inside the secret depths of my soul, Jesus guards my glass heart. Jesus won't let anything happen to it in the meantime.

And when I'm ready, he and I will gaze on its pain and beauty once again.

Part Two: Shattered

Chapter Six:
The Heights of Hope

It is hard to tell this part. I have talked about it, written about it, and lived through much traumatic re-experiencing of it. And still, sitting here trying to tell you of the hope I had, knowing better than anyone that Elliot died, it makes my chest tighten and my eyes well with tears. It shouldn't have happened. Some days, I don't know how to go back years and tell it.

Let Her Speak for Herself

So, I'll let the me who was pregnant with Elliot tell it. She was there. The me who'd just returned home from being admitted to the hospital overnight when Elliot's pregnancy was at just twenty-one weeks gestation. The me who was more convinced than ever that the baby I carried was a miracle promise from God. I returned home to an empty house. Dustin and Sylvia were on a mission trip to Juárez, and Valerie was spending the night at my parents' house.

I returned from my overnight stay at the hospital floating on a cloud of faith. I was convinced God had just given me the most complete, miraculous assurance I needed to be certain he had promised Elliot's life.

Blog Post: "He Who Has Promised"

Two months before

I sit on a hospital bed in a delivery room, a tiny incubator on my lap that contains an even tinier baby. My heart pounds with anxiety as I ask the nurse if my baby is okay. She nods, unconcerned, and touches him. He begins moving, and I feel his movement beneath my hand. He even sucks at my finger. He's alive! Alive! My heart rejoices. I give my baby a name: Promise.

When I awoke from the dream that November morning, I wept. It was so vivid, and it felt so cruel. I did not have a living baby. I had two babies who'd died within the previous nine months, miscarried in early pregnancy. Their little bodies were not warm and moving like the baby in my dream. They were buried under a tree on my parents' property.

Only as the morning progressed and the sadness and hurt dissipated did I begin to wonder about the dream. It reminded me of two other times in life when I truly believed God had told me something in a dream. I wrote in my journal that morning: *In the dream, I gave him a name: Promise. Or is that the name you gave him, Lord? What kind of promise are you giving me? I think you were in this dream.*

A month and a half later, an unexpectedly positive pregnancy test propelled my thoughts back to this dream. Fear of losing another baby almost immediately gripped me, except for the tiny whisper of hope, hope for my Promise.

I held my heart back from fully hoping for a baby and remained cautious. At seven weeks pregnant, when I first saw blood, I was crushed. I wept in the bathroom in the middle of the night, knowing what that amount of blood meant. For my last two pregnancies, it meant that my babies had died. As my husband held me, I cried, "I really thought this one was going to be different!" Completely devastated.

As a formality, I went to the doctor the next morning, expecting to hear that awful news: you've lost your baby. Instead, I heard a heartbeat. A heartbeat! My baby was alive! I sat in my car afterward, shaking with sobs, unable to drive, and barely able to talk to my husband about the joyous miracle that our baby was still alive! The echo of the Promise rang in my heart.

I hoped my pregnancy would be uneventful after this awful scare. I didn't know just how much I would come to rely on God's Promise in the coming weeks and months.

At eight weeks, just a week after my first scare, I again lost a heavy amount of blood. It was the day after Christmas, and as Christmas had fallen on a Sunday, this Monday, doctor's offices were closed. No doctor could see me, and as the bleeding began to subside, I knew it didn't warrant a trip to the emergency room. I would just have to wait. It was our day to celebrate Christmas with my family, and they were so generous and loving while I sat in a chair the entire day, paralyzed with dread and worry.

And yet. And yet! There was this tiny tether of hope, deep inside me, holding onto what I deeply wanted to be a Promise from God.

The next morning, again, my husband and I heard our baby's heartbeat and saw his tiny frame on the ultrasound machine. Alive! But what was going on?

Two days later, at my first "official" prenatal appointment, the doctor saw and diagnosed that I had a subchorionic bleed, a collection of blood in my uterus. She didn't say that day, but I'd come to find out in coming appointments and from other doctors just how massive the bleed was. It dwarfed the baby. More than one doctor has looked at original pictures of the bleed and called it "one of the biggest" they'd ever seen. The diagnosis was not the news I'd hoped to hear; my first miscarriage occurred right after I lost a lot of blood and was diagnosed with a subchorionic bleed as well. I prayed that this time, the bleed would dissolve and not cause any more external bleeding. That was not to be.

I experienced some spotting on and off after that but was hopeful as it did not usually amount to much. Then, around ten and a half weeks, I began having a heavier stream of blood. I didn't know when to head to the doctor. If it subsided, I'd try to remain calm. If it picked up, I'd panic. I'd tell God, "I want to believe your Promise! I want to believe!" But I also knew that I didn't always understand God's ways, and maybe his Promise meant something different than I wanted it to mean. I had doubts. I had fears.

And the evidence before my eyes did not give me a physical reason to hope. After a few days of on-and-off bleeding, it became a flood. I spent one day waiting for an afternoon doctor's appointment, and my mom came to help me with my two preschool-age girls. I wanted to get them out of the house, so I suggested we take them to McDonald's. As I sat there eating, I suddenly felt that heart-sinking feeling of warm fluid filling my pad. I ran to the bathroom. As I sat on the toilet, I couldn't believe what I was seeing: blood pouring out of me in a steady stream, like water. I sat there for probably five minutes, and the stream just continued. Finally, it subsided enough for me to get off the toilet. How could my baby possibly be okay?

But again, he was okay! When we went to the doctor and again saw him wiggling around on the ultrasound, it was so miraculous! The word "Promise" became embedded in my heart, becoming an anchor to hold on to amid the fear that swelled against me almost daily.

And then, at eleven weeks, we got the joyous news we were having a boy! I could not have been more surprised. I really thought we were having a girl. But I thought both my girls were boys, so I should have known better. Finding out his gender gave him yet another layer of reality in my mind. Almost immediately, I started looking at boy names. Only one boy's name seemed to fit: Elliot, which means "The Lord is my God." Truly, this child had been created and sustained by the Lord his God.

After that awful round of bleeding, I remember thinking, "Well, nothing could be worse than that." These are the things that we should probably not think.

At thirteen weeks, it became much worse. As I lay in bed on a Wednesday night, I felt yet another gush of blood. I began frequent trips to the bathroom, blood coming in heavier waves each time. In between gushes, I lay on my side in bed, and contractions began. I felt them every few minutes, my uterus painfully hardening. Then I'd rush to the bathroom to find more blood. In the moments I was laying down, I turned on "Though You Slay Me" by Shane & Shane. Though I deeply wanted to believe God would perform a miracle, I knew I was having contractions and that was positive evidence for a miscarriage. I tried to put my mind on trusting and loving God even if he did not save my baby. *Though you slay me, yet I will praise You. Though you take from me, I will bless your name. Though you ruin me, still I will worship. Sing a song to the One who's all I need.*

When I went to the bathroom and blood clots filled the toilet, I was sure it was the end. I wept in my husband's arms. I wept for the baby I thought was lost, loving him so deeply yet not being able to do anything to prevent losing him. I sat in the bathtub, thinking it wouldn't be long before I delivered him.

And, unbelievably, somewhere deep, deep inside me, the word "Promise" still gave me the tiniest spark of hope. It wasn't much, but

I couldn't let it go.

We went to the emergency room, knowing that's what a pregnant mother does when losing this amount of blood. A nice doctor said he was going to do an ultrasound. The exam room looked exactly like the one I'd been in a year earlier, where an ultrasound confirmed that I'd lost my little Avery Rose. The dread that covered me was palpable. Surely, this time, I had lost another baby.

Oh, the wave of relief that washed away that dread! There was our little Elliot, wiggling around on the ultrasound without a care in the world! Even as blood still poured from me, and contractions still tightened my uterus. *Alive!* God had been allowing me to go through such a trial, yet he continued to miraculously intervene in Elliot's life! How could I not believe he had promised me this baby? It felt like having my son back from the dead.

After the thirteenth week, things started to improve. The bleeding from that awful emergency room day tapered off, and I had a couple of weeks with nothing. Then, I'd spot some more for a few days. This became normal life. A few times, I had heavier bleeding. By my sixteen-week appointment, the baby was looking well, the subchorionic bleed was much smaller, and it was everything I could hope for. Another check of the baby after bleeding at eighteen weeks showed he continued to grow well.

At my twenty-week ultrasound with the high-risk obstetrician in maternal-fetal medicine, Elliot still looked healthy, surpassing the ninety-ninth percentile in size. But when the doctor came in after the tech had scanned me, he described something that looked a little odd on the ultrasound screen.

"Do you see how this is kind of cloudy? That's your amniotic fluid, and normally it would look black on the screen. It appears that blood from your subchorionic bleed has gotten into the amniotic fluid. That tells us that there is a weakening in the amniotic sac."

Hmm. That didn't sound so good, but they didn't seem too worried. The doctor did tell me of the increased risk of my water breaking early due to the sac being compromised by the subchorionic bleed. But he didn't seem overly concerned otherwise. When my husband asked him what I should be doing/not doing, he simply said, "Just listen to your body." Okay. Well, I would try to do that.

Later that very day, my body did tell me something, but I wasn't able to interpret it just yet. I lost more "blood," but this time, it was light brown in color, and very watery. But, since it dissipated within the next couple of hours, I didn't worry.

The same thing happened a couple of nights later. And a couple of nights after that. And a couple of nights after that. Finally, I emailed the high-risk doc and asked if this could be amniotic fluid leaking.

The day he returned my email, I had another loss of fluid overnight, and his email directed me to go in the next time it happened. I wanted more direction, so I also emailed my regular OB. Almost the moment she called me, I lost another gush of fluid. I told her what happened, and she said calmly, "Go to the hospital." So, I went.

The kind nurse there got me ready to see the doctor and wheeled in the ultrasound machine. When I told them I wasn't losing any more blood/fluid at the moment, no one seemed too concerned. The doctor pulled up the picture of Elliot on the ultrasound.

"Hmm. Your fluid does seem to be diminished. Sometimes this can be caused by not drinking enough water."

I told him how much water I drink. "Oh, you do," he replied. Guess that wasn't it.

I found out later that the amount of fluid he measured total in my uterus was 3.8 centimeters. The amount that should be measurable is at least eight centimeters.

Still, he didn't seem concerned. Maybe it was just a low amount of fluid for some reason. They did a test on me called "Amni-sure," in which they swabbed inside me for a sample of the fluid. Then they had to wait while the swab interacted with some chemical in a vial and turned a certain color. As the nurse waited with the vial in her hand, the doctor started talking about how it really looked more like mucous, and I could go right home if it was negative and—

"Actually, it's positive," the nurse interrupted him, holding up the vial.

The doctor's face abruptly changed. "Oh," he said. "I'm sorry." He and the nurse just looked at me as I cried a little. It was not what I wanted to hear. I know the prognosis for a woman's water breaking so early. It is not good. In truth, I didn't fully understand the gravity of this discovery. From their demeanor, it was like being told my baby had a terminal condition.

The doctor started talking about lots of things I could do/not do about the situation. He said that once (*once!*) he'd seen a woman's water break at nineteen weeks, and somehow the amniotic sac repaired itself and she went on to have her baby at thirty-five weeks. But that was the only example he could think of.

He talked about trying to do bed rest at home, but how that's really hard, but I could try to lay down at least two hours in the morning, afternoon, and evening…

He talked about how if the fluid didn't replenish, I'd have some hard decisions to make, as without fluid, the baby's lungs could not possibly develop, and even somewhere in there mentioned the possibility of "terminating the pregnancy."

He said they could keep me at the hospital for now, though there was nothing they could do…

Though I knew there was nothing they could do for a baby at twenty-one weeks gestation, for some reason, I felt compelled to stay at the hospital. They admitted me, and the sweet nurse kept hugging me and took me to a more "comfy bed," as she put it. I immediately contacted everyone I could think of to begin praying. And pray they did.

My mom told me later that she caught the nurse in the hall, and the nurse tried to reassure her a little, saying that she had seen these things turn around. My mom asked, "Like, how often? Fifty-fifty?" The nurse got serious.

"No," she said. "The odds aren't that good. Maybe eighty-twenty."

I felt strangely at peace, even as I battled fear and anxiety. Everything about what I was hearing and seeing on the medical professionals' faces was prognoses of doom. But I knew that my friends, family, and church were calling upon Jesus' name on behalf of Elliot. And I knew the miracles God had already performed on behalf of my little Promise. God is so much bigger than what man can see!

I rested throughout the night and didn't lose any more fluid.

By one p.m. the next day, Dr. Bozeman, my favorite doctor who had delivered Sylvia, came in and greeted me warmly. He sat in a chair to have the hard talk with me, again, about all the realistically grim things losing amniotic fluid could mean. Then, he went to the ultrasound machine to scan me.

As he scanned, he seemed pleasantly surprised.

"Oh, there's some fluid. Yeah, there's some more."

I could tell he was adding it all up. After he was done, he left for a while. When he came back, he said he had talked to one of the high-risk docs in maternal-fetal medicine.

"She's skeptical that your water really did break yesterday with as much fluid as you have today. But I told her that the results were very sure."

Already God's miracle had confounded medical science!

Dr. Bozeman talked a little more, and then sat down, kind of smiling and shaking his head. "It's just kind of contradictory…the amount of fluid you had yesterday compared to the amount you have today…but miracles do happen."

So that's why I felt compelled to stay overnight! These readings showed something beyond what medical science could explain, much more than would be reasonable to expect in a day, and I believe God wanted to show up. In less than twenty-four hours, my amniotic fluid had increased in measure from only 3.8 centimeters to more than nine!

Dr. Bozeman and I talked some more, and he was relieved and encouraged. I told him about all the people who'd been praying for me, and he nodded in agreement when I said that's what had done it. As he walked out the door, he told me one more time, "Your fluid levels today really are miraculous."

Miraculous. God had done it. For me. For Elliot. But mostly for the glory of his name, that all those prayer warriors, all those doctors and nurses, all those skeptics who might happen to see the post on Facebook, would give glory to him who is able to do immeasurably more than all we ask or imagine.

As I've recalled the roller coaster of this pregnancy, I know during the low points, I wondered, *Why is this happening to me? After losing two babies, why couldn't this pregnancy just be uneventful?*

But I've also started asking that question in a different way: *Why is this happening* for *me? Why did God bless me with a prophetic dream of hope and encouragement? Why did every episode of bleeding result in a baby whose heart still beat? Why did Elliot survive contractions and loss of blood clots? Why should I receive a miracle of healing in my amniotic fluid?*

Because God. That's all there is. I don't know why he sometimes gives and sometimes takes away. I don't know what twists and turns this pregnancy will take from here. I don't know what joys and challenges Elliot's life may bring.

But I know my God. And I know that no miracle could occur without a need born out of distress. It's like when the disciples asked Jesus about the man born blind, and who had sinned to cause him to be that way. Jesus answered, "It was not that this man sinned, or his parents, but that the works of God might be displayed in him." I am humbled that the works of God have been displayed in me.

Does that mean I want this roller coaster to continue? No, thanks! But if God wills it so that his name will receive more glory, I will take it.

I will also take this sweet life God has entrusted to me, and guard it well. The doctors may say I'm fine and may clear me to return to "normal activity"—but it is my season to rest. Rest my body. Rest my heart. Rest in Jesus. I will let all those kind people in my life who offer to help me, help. I'll let go of the guilt of not cleaning or shopping or cooking or taking the girls to all sorts of places. There will be plenty of time for that in life. Today, I cherish and protect Elliot's little life inside me, not taking for granted the miracles God has performed on his behalf.

He who has *promised* is faithful.

***

Looking Back

It makes me a little sick to read how I flippantly utilized that blind man passage from John to justify my "suffering" for God's glory. That's the kind of thing I really hate now.

Oh, and that verse "He who is promised is faithful" comes from Hebrews 10:23, referring to God's promises to us who have an inheritance in Christ, and to the heroes of old who believed God.

I didn't even look it up in context but grabbed it to align with what I desperately hoped for and wanted. However, this verse sits in a context I did not think of while I sat in my certainty. In Hebrews 11:13, the writer states, "These all died in faith, *not* having received the things promised, but having seen them and greeted them from afar, and having acknowledged that they were strangers and exiles on the earth (emphasis added)."

Would I have let myself believe that? That Elliot would *not* be a promise fulfilled like I thought he would be? Would I have allowed myself to believe I would die in faith, *not* receiving the thing promised until eternity?

I couldn't have let my mind linger there for one moment, no.

And more full disclosure: I now intensely dislike that Shane & Shane song, "Though You Slay Me." Okay, and one more confession: when I had the dream of a baby named Promise, it was a baby girl. This was why I was so surprised when my blood test told us Elliot was a boy. I didn't share that with anyone, though. I changed it to a boy when I retold the dream. I had to make God's promise fit my current reality.

But so much hope had been realistic, logical even. A doctor had just stated that my fluid levels were miraculous. Certainly, my faith was not foolish. I had so much reason to hope and to trust. And, in the end, I am a mommy. I will *always* hope for the best for my children, no matter the odds or dire predictions. I will fight for them, I will fight for them, I will fight for them. And in this brief and beautiful season of my life, fighting for him meant hope.

But then hope became a confusing jumble of contradictions. Again, I will let a different me tell it, this time two months after Elliot had died. This is an excerpt from a very long narrative I wrote of my journey with Elliot. I submitted this testimonial to a website called "Faces of Loss, Faces of Hope," an amazing platform to give bereaved parents a space to share the stories of their beloved babies. This is what happened after the "miracle" of finding more fluid than Dr. Bozeman expected.

A Maybe Not Miracle?

From my testimony on Faces of Loss, Faces of Hope, written two months after

Two days later, though, I returned to the hospital one more time after having another gush of fluid. I got mixed messages about what was now being seen. The test for amniotic fluid came back negative this time. But when the doctor scanned me to check my fluid level, he said, "There is less fluid than two days ago. Markedly less."

What did that mean? I figured this is why God had given me a promise, something to hold on to through all the highs and lows of this rocky pregnancy. The next day I had an appointment with the high-risk doctor in maternal-fetal medicine, where I hoped to receive more answers.

I expected the doctor to find plenty of fluid, for him to brush me off as I'd felt brushed off most of the pregnancy. I thought I'd go home annoyed that they weren't very concerned about me. I was not worried.

So when, at the appointment on March 31, the high-risk OB started talking about options for how to now proceed in the pregnancy, it took me some time to comprehend. There was not plenty of fluid anymore. He didn't even measure it. He just said, "There are some pockets, but yes, your water has broken." Then he delicately asked what kind of lengths we wanted to go to in order to save our baby. I said, "We want to do everything we can."

The doctor said I could be admitted to the hospital ten days later, at twenty-two weeks and five days, and then they would start me on steroid shots and two days' worth of antibiotics. Twenty-three weeks is the earliest they would medically intervene in saving Elliot's life if he was born. The doctor said, "We will keep you until the baby is born. If you haven't delivered by thirty-four weeks, we will induce you then. You could be in the hospital a very long time."

I also vaguely remember him mentioning that fluid was necessary to develop Elliot's lungs. "We won't know until he is born if his lungs have developed enough for him to survive. You could carry him all the way to forty weeks, but if his lungs don't develop, he still might not make it."

I didn't like that. I tucked it away in a corner of my mind and have only pulled it back out now in retrospect. At least I can say the doctor warned me that what happened could happen.

I called my husband as I drove home, and that's when it hit me, and I cried. Potentially eleven weeks in the hospital? I had two little girls to take care of! How were we going to do this? And yet, I had to take care of Elliot.

I continued the next nine days on strict bedrest at home. My girls would crawl into bed with me and color, read, or watch TV. I held them close, knowing I'd be leaving them soon.

I also got on a PPROM (Preterm Premature Rupture of Membranes) Facebook group and read "happy ending" stories. I found the American Association of PPROM website and read an encouraging study posted there. Looking back, I only used these two sources to inform my knowledge of PPROM and the potential risks to my baby. Between my "promise" from God and these encouraging stories, I let myself believe entirely I would walk out of the hospital one day with Elliot in my arms.

The day before I was supposed to be admitted to the hospital, I awoke to the heaviest bleeding I'd experienced during the whole pregnancy. It overflowed my pad, soaking my pants to my ankles. It was horrifying. I thought, *No! I can't lose this baby the day before I'm supposed to go to the hospital!* Looking back, I think that perhaps my amniotic sac finally broke, an entire loss of fluid mixed with blood.

As my husband drove us to the hospital, I cried. I sat in a daze, hoping, and praying that God would continue his promise of protection over Elliot's life. Would he even be alive when we got there?

Again, he was alive! The woman who would become my high-risk OB in the hospital was so encouraged that I was no longer bleeding. Elliot bounced around on the ultrasound screen as always. But the doctor once again did not go to the trouble of trying to measure the fluid. She said, "There's a little pocket of fluid around his face, and that's encouraging."

Oh, how I believed all this was part of God's promise! Elliot was still alive! And though there was hardly any fluid, the place where there was fluid seemed to be right where he needed it: around his face, where he could breathe it.

That day, April 9, I was admitted to St. Joseph's Hospital. They gave me steroid shots and IV antibiotics to protect me against infection. A doctor from the NICU came to have a talk with my husband and me about the scary statistics were we to have Elliot as an "extremely premature baby" (twenty-three weeks). He was grim. I tried not to let his hopeless realism get to me. I remember saying to him, "I hope I don't see you for several more weeks!"

To which he replied without humor, "That would be outrageous." Ouch. He didn't think I'd be pregnant much longer.

But I was already beating statistics. From what I've read, most women go into labor within forty-eight hours of their water breaking. I'd already been leaking fluid for three weeks, and now my water had completely broken. Every day I went on without developing an infection or going into labor, I beat the odds. And the days and weeks did go by. Twenty-four weeks. Twenty-five. Twenty-six. Twenty-seven. Twenty-eight! Odds for a premature baby went up dramatically after twenty-eight weeks. Again, I let myself be encouraged by those statistics and every positive story. The study on the PPROM website said that for women who remained pregnant a certain number of weeks after having PPROM between 18-24 weeks, survival rates for babies were ninety percent! I just *knew* Elliot would be okay!

I have since read two studies that give much bleaker statistics. One found that survival rates are only fifty percent if a woman's water breaks while her baby is pre-viable. Another study showed a survival rate of ten percent.

Just studies. People's stories ultimately don't account for the fact that there is a God in heaven who numbers the days of all people. Why do some babies live and some die? This is the question all of us bereaved mothers grapple with.

But while I was pregnant, I let the studies and stories buoy my hope: One mom on the Facebook group who PPROM-ed at seventeen weeks with no measurable fluid gave birth to a perfectly healthy baby! Another one whose doctor said her baby had a one-percent chance of survival showed us a picture of her now-healthy two-year-old! Story after story of hope. And when, well, one mom here and there shared with our group that she lost her baby, it was so sad. I shed tears. And then (I can't believe this), I would feel awash with gratitude that that wasn't going to happen to me.

Well-meaning friends and family often told me of a person they knew whose son or cousin or nephew had been born at twenty-six, twenty-five, or twenty-four weeks and was now a 280-pound linebacker or something. Now, these stories break my heart and feed my anger, but back then, they just proved that Elliot would be okay.

In the hospital, as the days and weeks went by, I had a few instances of bleeding that had me moved to the Labor and Delivery department to be put on continuous monitoring and on a magnesium drip to protect Elliot's brain. This first happened just a week after being admitted. It happened again over Mother's Day weekend when I was twenty-seven weeks and three days. I had some contractions, and the doctor checked my cervix. One centimeter. Definitely not in labor. But I was so thankful I was there in the hospital, believing God planned to bring his dream of my promised Elliot alive and healthy, though premature in an incubator, to fruition. He had me in the best place to care for Elliot and me.

Being away from my family was the hardest part of being in the hospital. It was stressful and traumatic in many ways, but we all knew that it would have been worth it once we had Elliot at home. They visited several times a week, and we found ways to make the best of our situation, having fun in my hospital room, the courtyard outside, or in the hospital cafeteria.

The best part of being in the hospital was my uninterrupted time with Elliot. Oh, how I fell in love with him! I listened to his precious heartbeat for an hour each morning and each evening, felt his movements, and got to notice them because I wasn't chasing around two preschoolers like I would have been if I'd been at home. I was so used to the feeling of him, especially since, without fluid, he couldn't move freely in my belly. He was in a transverse position the entire time I was in the hospital. I knew where every part of his body was. I talked to him and sang to him and prayed for him, but I wish I had done it more. I took for granted that I would have a lifetime with him, so I worried about other things. I wanted to be productive, so I read books, paid bills, ordered groceries for my family, and completed professional development for my teaching license.

If I had known that was my only time with him, I would have just sat each day with my hands on my belly, relishing every moment and every movement.

***

I'll stop there. You know what's coming. Reading it, I see that even those couple of months after Elliot died, my theological assumptions were still so ingrained. "There is a God in heaven who numbers the days of all people." Really? I really thought God was sitting up in heaven ticking off Elliot's very few days? No wonder I was struggling.

It was the only way I knew how to have faith. And this method of faith had worked through life's previous hardships and unanswered questions. We all have times we are certain we understand life's mysteries. I remember when I was enduring the scary pregnancy with Elliot, a woman in my Bible study prayed over me, saying, "I want you to know God has put on my heart that your body is not failing. He has a plan for Elliot's life, and he will be a testimony to God's strength in adversity." There it is again. The Plan.

Another friend, after I told her about the dream in which I'd had a tiny baby named Promise, called just to say, "I just have to tell you what the Lord brought to mind! That his promises never come without a struggle!"

It felt like a mystical wonder, and all I had to do to was truly believe for this plan and promise of God to work out. And to me, it could only work out if Elliot lived. I thought so incredibly much that nothing could undo this plan, this promise of God.

But trauma unravels certainty. Death shakes all assumptions.

Chapter Seven:
From Dream to Nightmare

If somehow I've misunderstood your promise, and my son dies, I feel like I'll die too. —March 31

God, I love sweet Elliot more than I can say. Cause him to develop normally despite the lack of fluid. I trust your will to bring about Elliot's life as you fulfill your promise and bring glory to your name. —April 30

I hate admitting this, but I have to get it out to you so Satan can't use it: the death of other babies makes me doubt your goodness. It brings fear into me that you'll allow Elliot to die, too. And I don't know what to do with that fear except just bring it to you. I'm just desperate to hold my baby in my arms, to kiss his little face, to bring him home and watch him grow. And even with the promise you've given and the miraculous ways you've preserved his life, that fear of losing him can creep back in... Just fulfill your promise for little Elliot, Lord. Let that fluid flow in just the right way so he keeps breathing it and ingesting it and that his lungs and every other system just miraculously form... God, I pray the miraculous for my boy! —May 16

I am precious to you! Elliot is precious to you! Thank you for this miracle of pregnancy, for feeling him squirm and kick. And you are there with him, Lord! You know every secret thing that's going on in my womb, and you know how to form his lungs even without fluid. I don't know why some little babies don't get to see days on this earth, Jesus, but I'm confident that Elliot will. In your book are written all the days you've formed for him. I can't wait to meet and hold my son. —May 25

***

It's hard to think back to those seven weeks I spent in the hospital, waiting, hoping, trying to share my faith, and fighting my fear. I don't know the longest you've spent in the hospital, and there are many people who've endured a much longer stay than fifty days. But time really slowed in there. The sights, smells, and sounds in hospitals and even doctors' offices can instantly take me back there. It's all imprinted. The nurses who loved me, the sweet cleaning lady who chatted with me in Spanish, and all the friends and family who filled my days with visits. Rarely did a day pass without one of my friends visiting. My dear friend and college roommate Megan even flew out from Ohio near the beginning of my stay to help at my house, drive my girls from place to place, bring me items from home, and just be with me. It was a unique time, a holy time, I think.

Dustin brought the girls a couple of times a week. My mom carted them to see me another couple of times per week. They were so sweet and understanding, just four-and-a-half and going on three years old. They played with toys and colored. We'd sometimes tie a string across the room and play balloon volleyball. The nurses knew them by name. I wrote them little storybooks and crocheted mini blankets for their dolls. The nurses brought me the oversized wheelchair so Sylvia and Valerie could snuggle in on either side of me while Dustin wheeled us down to the cafeteria, Elliot snugly in the middle of me in the middle of his sisters. The hospital cafeteria food was surprisingly tasty; I always ordered the deluxe grilled cheese. There's a little courtyard outside the cafeteria with big outdoor rocking chairs. I'd sit in those chairs, a welcome relief from my wheelchair, and watch my lively girls run and play. I remember rocking and thinking, "I'm rocking my baby inside my tummy now, but I can't wait to rock him at home when he's outside my tummy!"

Even with all the support and encouragement from friends and family, I felt guilty that I was lounging around in the hospital while everyone else was raising my kids for me. And yet I knew I had to do it. I just let myself focus on the day Elliot would be born alive, probably with an extended NICU stay to endure, but then I'd imagine the day we'd bring him home. It would be the biggest party of our family's life. That picture kept me from despair.

What Actually Happened

I will let a newly bereaved me continue the story. It was freshest in her mind, though it has never left mine. I must live most days without dwelling on these details in order to function. But each detail matters because each second of my son's precious earthly life matters.

Continued from my contribution to Faces of Loss, Faces of Hope, submitted two months after Elliot died.

As my time in the hospital progressed, a few things began to happen. Occasionally I started having contractions. Sometimes, I'd have "bright red" bleeding, which jumped my medical team into action because of the concern that red bleeding could signal a placental abruption. Occasionally, Elliot's heart rate would dip while I was on the monitor, a concern because babies with no fluid can more easily lay on their cord and compress it. Again, I was just so thankful I was in a place where God would use the medical team to keep Elliot and me safe.

When I was twenty-nine weeks and two days, my friend Kate visited and had lunch with me in my hospital room. I felt some leakage on my pad and excused myself to the bathroom, where I saw a bright red blood clot for the first time. I called my nurse. She looked at it and immediately wrapped my belly with straps to put Elliot on the fetal heart rate monitor. Kate stayed, and we continued chatting and started laughing about something. My nurse ran in. I thought my laughing had slipped Elliot off the monitor, but after listening, I realized his regular 150-160 beats-per-minute heartbeat was thumping much slower. 100. 90. 80. I covered my face and started crying.

My nurse called something over the speaker and shifted me to my side. Elliot's heart rate was still slow. Suddenly a dozen doctors and nurses were in my room, including my high-risk OB. Then they disconnected my bed from the wall and ran me to Labor and Delivery. They hooked me up to the monitor again, and Elliot's heart rate was coming back up. Everyone breathed a sigh of relief. I stayed the weekend in Labor and Delivery on magnesium, prohibited from eating and drinking, and continuously monitored with straps on my belly measuring any small contractions and every beat of Elliot's heart. Forty-eight hours of the rhythmic whooshing proved my son was alive inside me. Looking back, what a lucky mommy I was to have hours and hours on end like that, with Elliot's heartbeat as my comforting background noise. How desperately I wish I could hear that heartbeat again. I miss it.

Yet again, this instance would confirm that God continued to perform miracles on Elliot's behalf. *What if my nurse had not put me on the monitor? What if I had been downstairs in the cafeteria? Elliot could have compressed his cord and died!* But, of course, God promised this child. Therefore, he would always take care of Elliot.

I had some considerable contractions over that weekend. There were a few hours when the contractions were regular and painful. I called my husband and told him to pack a bag. The doctors hesitated to check my cervix because of the infection risk to a PPROM patient. Finally, they did, but it was just two centimeters and showed no signs of active labor. The contractions subsided, and they once again returned me to my antepartum room a couple of days later, on a Sunday morning. I was preparing myself to be in the hospital for the long haul, all the way to thirty-four weeks. I was very tired of being away from my family. I even struggled with wishing Elliot would just come. Now I am ashamed of thinking that. In my belly, Elliot was safe. In my belly, Elliot was alive. Every day I had with him was a miracle. But since I "knew" he would live, I had a hard time appreciating being pregnant. Yet, I would always think, *God will take him out when it's safer for him out than in*. I just wanted my baby to be okay. I would endure anything for that to happen. And I trusted God's wisdom to cause all the details to work out exactly as they were supposed to.

The next day, Memorial Day, Monday, May 29, when I was twenty-nine weeks and five days and had been in the hospital for exactly fifty days, I awoke to a contraction and a little more bleeding. The doctor on call moved me back to Labor and Delivery. I remember being disappointed that I wouldn't get to eat, so I scarfed a granola bar in secret before they moved me. I lay in the Labor and Delivery room on continuous monitoring, and they decided not to put me on magnesium just yet because my bleeding was not very bad. Every time the nurse would check my pad, she'd say, "Oh, there's not much there." I thought it was just another precautionary day, and I'd be back in antepartum before too long.

Around nine a.m., I started having contractions that felt like the ones I'd had over the weekend. They were painful, in my lower back, and I had to breathe through them. But they weren't regular. Ten minutes apart. Twenty minutes. Thirty minutes. Eight minutes. All over the place. At one point, I felt Elliot moving like crazy and wondered if he could've changed position. The doctor and nurse kept checking on me, but none of us worried about what was going on. Around noon, the doctor said if I was still having contractions in an hour, she'd check my cervix. She also said she wanted to do an ultrasound to check Elliot's position. The nurse gave me Tylenol and a heating pad for my back. I kept myself busy paying bills of all things, writing down when I had a "strong" contraction, and listening to my baby's beautiful heartbeat.

My nurse came in around 2:30 and I told her the contractions were getting more uncomfortable and I'd like the doctor to check me. Then many things happened all at once. I felt a low contraction, almost like I had to push. The doctor came in with the ultrasound machine. The nurse told her about my contraction. The doctor did a quick ultrasound and said, "Oh, the baby has changed position!" He'd gone from transverse to breech just that morning. Then the doctor checked my cervix. She calmly (almost too calmly) looked at the nurse and said, "Okay, she's at like nine centimeters."

What? *Nine centimeters?!*

Then it all went haywire. I was in the middle of comprehending this, asking her what was going to happen; she told me we'd move toward a C-section and probably had time to put me on a spinal so I could be awake. I called my husband, and then…

Elliot's heart rate plummeted down to the sixties. It was more terrifying than I can describe. Suddenly, the nurse was calling over the intercom and disconnecting my bed from the wall. A half dozen people filled the room, and they sprinted me down the hall. I closed my eyes and prayed, "Jesus, Jesus, Jesus." I put my life and Elliot's life in the hands of the Lord.

Then I was in an operating room, hands all over me, preparing me for surgery, someone rubbing my belly I think to stimulate Elliot. It was so awful. I don't think I have yet really processed how traumatic Elliot's birth was. I heard someone say, "You're going to sleep now."

And the next thing I remember was someone saying, "Heidi. Heidi." I opened my eyes and was in a recovery room with a doctor and a nurse and my husband. I felt so awful. The doctor asked, "How do you feel?" And all I could croak out was, "My throat hurts."

But I just wanted to know about Elliot. My Elliot! My baby whom I had been fighting for the past six and a half months, the past nine weeks on bed rest, seven in the hospital. *How was Elliot?* All I cared about was him.

Then my wonderful husband was at my side holding up his phone with a picture of my baby boy, Elliot William, *alive*, and holding my husband's finger with his perfect little hand.

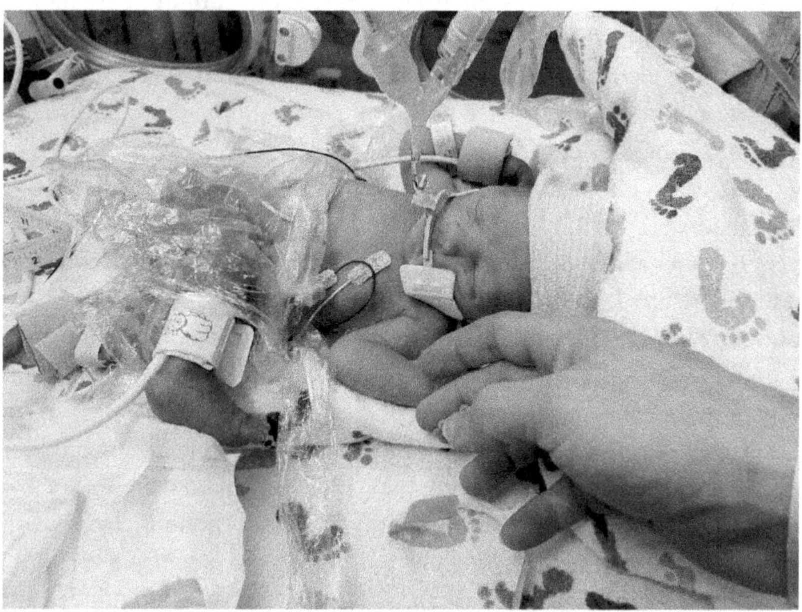

Relief flooded me. It got even better when they told me he was three pounds, fourteen ounces. What a big baby for only thirty weeks! We'd made it! I truly thought all the worst was over. Finally, my baby was here. And even if our lives would now involve weeks or months with a baby in the NICU, it didn't matter. God had delivered Elliot from a broken pregnancy in my broken body. His promise really must've been true. It breaks my heart now to remember how perfectly content and happy I was. I pictured our lives with Elliot, with my girls having a little brother. My husband and I gave all credit and glory to God and continued to trust God's promise that Elliot would live. I remember preparing myself for ups and downs in the NICU, and I knew I would hold on to God's promise to help me through those times.

My husband left me so he could be with Elliot, and I anxiously awaited news about when I would get to meet my son. My husband and I texted back and forth, and he told me that the doctors were having a hard time getting Elliot's oxygen levels stable. It was scary, and I turned to the Lord to help me not to fear. I posted updates on Facebook and asked everybody to pray. I wanted a miracle, somewhere in all this, for God to do something that doctors couldn't explain and would prove that God was the one sustaining Elliot! Perhaps God had always intended all these complications so he could show his glory and we could share Christ with people who didn't know him. *How special Elliot is to God,* I thought!

After a couple hours, my husband came back with the doctor who had delivered Elliot and had been working on him. She was very somber. She said that everything indicated Elliot's lungs were underdeveloped, that his left lung was inflated, but his right lung was not. Air was leaking into his chest cavity, creating something called a pneumothorax. They were going to put in a chest tube to drain the air and help his right lung inflate. She said that she didn't know if his lungs were developed enough for him to live, and only time would tell if they were. Oh, I hated hearing that. I had so hoped that God would develop his lungs despite the lack of fluid. But, I thought, *This is how God is going to show his glory: by fulfilling his promise for Elliot's life despite the difficulties with his lungs*. I heard her and nodded my understanding but would not even let my mind consider the worst possibility. Elliot was alive, and he would stay alive.

Finally, almost six hours after he'd been born, I was allowed to see him. The chest tube helped, along with putting him on nitrous oxide, and his oxygen levels were stable. First, my nurse took me to see him in my bulky hospital bed. But there was not space in his little NICU room. I couldn't get close enough to really see him, let alone touch him. So, I asked her to take me back and help me get in a wheelchair. She did, and it was hard. My midsection all the way from my groin to my shoulders felt like someone had beaten me with a baseball bat. Every time I elevated my head from a laying position, I'd get dizzy and on the verge of passing out. I was still connected to an IV, a catheter, and an oxygen tube. But nothing mattered compared to being with my son! And it was all worth it as I put my hands in the incubator and touched him for the first time. He opened his sweet eyes and looked at me. He wrapped his little fingers around my finger. My heart was full.

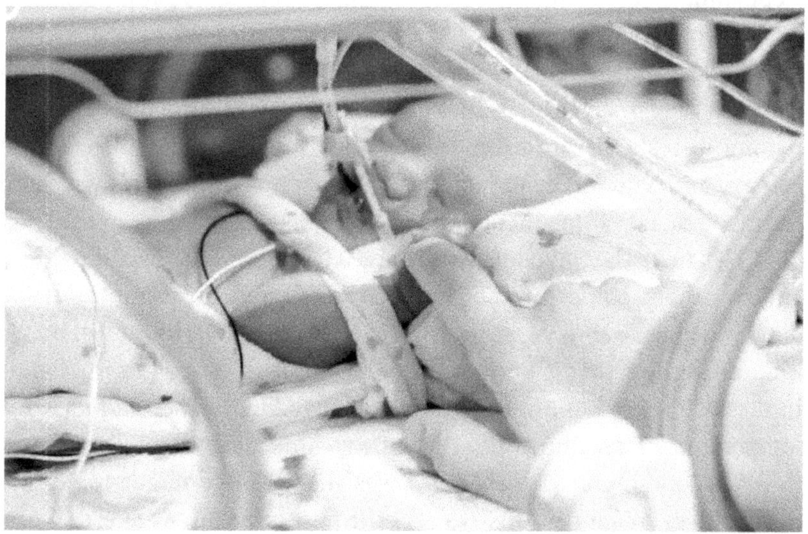

After only fifteen minutes, I broke into a sweat and almost passed out. I had lost a lot of blood during delivery. They took me back to my antepartum room for the night. I was sad my first moments with him were so short, but it was okay. Now that he was here, now that his oxygen was stable, I truly believed there was nothing to fear. I went to bed that night more concerned with getting myself feeling better so I could really start mothering him.

I remained awake all night in constant pain, but so deliriously happy about having my little boy. The nurse tried a couple times to have me sit up and try to stand, but anytime I'd even sit up, I would almost pass out. By morning, they decided I should have a blood transfusion. This meant more time away from my Elliot. But I kept thinking, *just get better and then I can really start spending time with him!* My husband spent the most time with him that Tuesday, May 30, when Elliot was one day old. I finally got my blood transfusion that afternoon, and it took a while. After it was done and they checked to see if I could stand a little, they disconnected me from my IV and catheter. It was that afternoon when Elliot was already over twenty-four hours old that I finally got to see him again. I sang to him. I cradle-held him in the incubator. But after only forty-five minutes with him, I felt so sick again, so I went back to my room. I finally slept some. *Just recover, get better,* I kept thinking. Of course, now, I wish I would've spent every single moment with him. I had no idea.

My husband went home, and my amazing sister-in-law Sarah came to stay the night. I spent more time with him that evening, feeling refreshed from a little sleep. But I was still exhausted from surgery and pain medication and had so much discomfort. It was hard for me to stand by his incubator for very long.

The next day, Wednesday, May 31, Elliot was two days old, and my mom came to meet him. I wish I could remember all the details of his few days in the NICU with more clarity, but they all kind of run together. I know I just spent a lot of time with my hands in the incubator, humming to him. I changed his diaper and took his temperature. I fed him little bits of my milk on a swab. My breast milk was coming in so well, and I was such a proud mama to be able to take care of him in this way. I still felt weak on Wednesday and would go back to my room to recover often. My husband returned and stayed the night.

By Thursday, June 1, Elliot's third day of life, I was finally starting to feel a little better. My sweet husband headed home that day. He had a vasectomy scheduled for the next day, of all things. We'd discussed it months before, and both agreed we couldn't endure any more pregnancy trauma and loss, and we needed permanent birth control. When Elliot was unexpectedly born that week, we talked about if he should reschedule the surgery. But Elliot was so stable, and we decided it was actually a "good" time to do it, since the girls were already cared for by grandparents, and Elliot and I were stable in the hospital. That Thursday morning, my sweet husband Dustin said goodbye to Elliot, and told him, "I'll see you next week!" He planned to return Sunday if he felt good enough. But that was the last time he saw Elliot alive. I cannot express how much it has broken both of our hearts that he didn't get to see Elliot during his last two days of life. There's no way we could've known.

I spent considerable time that day trying to do some walking. My girls came for one last visit to the hospital, but they were not allowed in the NICU to meet Elliot because it was technically still flu season. No one under the age of eighteen was admitted. This also has made me very sad; they were on the same floor as their living, breathing baby brother, just a few walls away! But they never saw him wiggle, never touched his warm skin. The only time they ever saw their baby brother was in a coffin.

Other family members visited that day, and I spent lots of time with my boy. They tried turning off his chest tube to see if his pneumothorax had healed. He did fine at first, but at eight p.m. that night, his heart rate and oxygen levels dipped majorly, and they turned the chest tube back on. He stabilized. It was a scary several minutes watching those critical numbers fall as the doctors tried to assess what to do. But I knew God had given me his promise to help me through those scary times. I remember Elliot's nurse telling me I did a really great job staying calm. I think I told her that I was praying and trusting God for Elliot's life.

The next day, Friday, June 2, Elliot's fourth day of life, there was a lot of paperwork to do as I was officially getting discharged from the hospital. After almost eight weeks! I was overjoyed. There were boarding rooms right next to the NICU I'd get to stay in for three more nights. I couldn't wait to be closer to my little guy. And I was finally feeling better! Except my feet had just begun to swell like balloons.

Once all the paperwork was done, and I was discharged, I moved into my boarding room and spent so much wonderful time with my little guy. He continued to be stable, though his oxygen need had gone up slightly over the past two days. I wasn't worried; this was all part of the NICU roller coaster I'd heard about. I was so ready to become a NICU mama. I was going to become an expert in all things Elliot and all things NICU—I just knew it. More visitors came that evening,

Elliot's grandma on my husband's side, and my brother-in-law and his wife, sharing the news with an adorable onesie that Elliot was going to be a big cousin! Yay! Another baby in the family to grow up with Elliot! Truly, if happiness was something tangible, it would've filled the room right then.

I stayed up late with Elliot and delivered him some milk in the middle of the night. I feel guilty now that I slept until eight in the morning of June 3, his fifth day of life, and didn't get to him until nine. But, of course, I just thought that the more I recovered, the better I would be for Elliot.

My memory of him that morning is one of the sweetest I have. There were no visitors, and he was stable. It was just Elliot and Mommy. The nurse had put little blue mitts on his hands to keep him from pulling at his cords. My feet hurt from the swelling, but I stood there the best I could. He grasped fingers on both my hands with his little hands. He'd grimace when I tried to pull away (thinking I'd put my feet up for a while), so I pulled up a chair and got as comfortable as I could. I sat there with him for at least an hour, maybe an hour and a half, my fingers in his mitt-wrapped hands, humming to him over and over again. I wonder now if he knew this was his last day, and if he was giving his mommy a special time to remember.

The roller coaster began again soon after that. Around eleven, his heart rate and blood pressure were dipping. There's a kind of fear where you just let yourself go numb, and that's where I went. Many medical professionals filled in his NICU room. I tried to stay calm, tried to pray, tried to hold on to God's promise. They did an x-ray and found that his chest tube had stopped working (probably clogged), so his pneumothorax was huge, and his right lung was not working. They immediately put in a new chest tube. He stabilized. The self-protective numbness gave way to warm gratitude as I praised God.

The doctor showed me the x-ray of Elliot's lungs, showing how greatly the pneumothorax had affected his internal organs, and that it had probably been pushing up against his heart, which was what caused the drops in heart rate, and also why the nurse couldn't hear any movement in his bowels when she checked. My poor baby! Oh, it hurt me to know there were all these complications going on inside his perfect-looking little body. But I asked the doctor why his oxygen didn't drop during that time—after all, a whole lung hadn't been working. The doctor said, "I don't know. It doesn't make sense."

But it made sense to me! It was clearly another miracle from God, which I proclaimed on Facebook to the hundreds of prayer warriors who loved little Elliot.

My big brother Ryan was the last of the family to meet Elliot, and he came that afternoon. Within all the craziness of the morning, I hadn't taken any pictures of Elliot that day. The only pictures I have of him alive from his last day are kind of blurry ones from my brother's cell phone.

All week, Elliot had little "sunglasses" on to protect his eyes from the light they shined on him for his jaundice. The only time I had seen his eyes was briefly on the night of his birth. As my brother and sister-in-law were getting ready to leave, the nurse said they were ready to turn off the light and take off his glasses. Yay! I would finally get to know my baby's face. He was so stinkin' cute. The nurse gave me a little breast milk to feed him on a swab. I put some in his mouth, and he just popped his eyes open to look at me. The three of us giggled as quietly as we could. It was just so cute. Again and again, every time I put the breast milk in his mouth, he popped his little eyes open. They were dark and beautiful and clear.

Why, oh why, did none of us think to take some pictures or a movie of that moment? I guess because we all believed there'd be hundreds more of those moments to come.

Around four that afternoon, after my brother had left, I was wiped out. I had just finished pumping my breast milk. The nurse said that Elliot and I could both use a nap. I agreed. I headed back to my boarding room after telling my little guy I'd be back soon.

How I wish I'd never left him.

Blog Post: "I Am Job's Wife"

Five months after

I think I, like most Christians, have lived under the possibly arrogant assumption that nothing could truly shake my faith. Most certainly, nothing could ever cause me to lose my faith. I have walked with God too long, been too close to Jesus, to ever truly doubt his love, power, or his very existence.

In the past five months, I have doubted all those things, certainties I never believed I could question. I have been, after all, a follower of Jesus Christ since I was fifteen years old. Christian college. Mission work. Teaching at a Christian school. All the "right" things, of course. What could cause such a crisis of faith for me?

Some people would assume these doubts of mine are caused by losing my five-day-old infant son, Elliot. Perhaps those people would think I am asking God, "Why? Why my baby? Why did you let him die?" And it's true. I ask those unanswerable questions every day.

But the reason for my doubts goes deeper than Elliot's death. The reason for my doubt is because of my great faith.

I think I am like a lot of Western Christians in the fact that, while I believe God can still perform miracles, I have never really witnessed one. Yes, I have heard about cancer patients whose cancer inexplicably went away, stories of miracles from overseas. I've seen lives changed and believed with all my heart that God's intervention in those lives was miraculous. But I, with my own eyes, have never seen a nature-defying miracle.

So, it took me a while to believe what I thought I was hearing from God was true. I had a dream of a baby in an incubator, a living baby whom I named "Promise." After two miscarriages that broke my heart, I wanted to believe God could be promising me something that could help me heal. I didn't know what that might be, or if, in fact, it was just a dream.

When I got pregnant a month after the dream, I hoped God had a promise to fulfill for me. But who am I to demand anything of God? I didn't set my hope fully on this promise; I didn't want to be presumptuous. I didn't claim to know what God was going to do. I remember thinking that if I miscarried, I would have to re-evaluate that dream and figure it wasn't from God or meant something else; God couldn't lie. If I misunderstood something, the fault would have to be with me, not with God.

As the pregnancy progressed, those months became difficult, scary, and unpredictable. I know of pregnancies in which the parents find out their sweet baby has birth defects or a condition that is "incompatible with life." I cannot imagine the trial of carrying a precious child and knowing that the baby would die shortly after birth. But my story is that I had a perfectly healthy baby growing inside while enduring a perfectly flawed pregnancy. Elliot could have lived if not for the issues in my pregnancy, in my broken womb. This haunts me.

Everything that could go wrong in my pregnancy did go wrong. The details of just how wrong are chronicled elsewhere, but suffice it to say, we thought on at least a half-dozen occasions we'd lost Elliot. Yet, every time the doctor put that cold gel and ultrasound wand on my belly, there was our boy, growing and feeling fine.

I believed that God gave me verses to hold on to during these scary times. One was Isaiah 41:10, which is also a line in the hymn "How Firm a Foundation." I would sing it to myself through my tears as my body poured blood at eleven weeks, or I writhed from contractions at thirteen weeks, or I lay on a hospital bed at twenty-one weeks, hearing the news my water had broken. *Fear not, I am with thee, O be not dismayed; for I am thy God and will still give thee aid. I'll strengthen thee, help thee, and cause thee to stand, upheld by my righteous, omnipotent hand.* Over and over, I sang it. Over and over, I felt God's comfort and that word: Promise.

I grew in faith that God not only did give me a promise for Elliot's life but that he wanted me to hold fast to that promise through any challenges we would face.

When I learned that my water had broken so early, that I would be hospitalized, and that Elliot would be delivered early, the dream seemed even less like "just a dream." I really was going to have a baby in an incubator. And, in my dream, despite my fears, my baby was alive. How could I not believe that this, too, would come to pass?

Oh, what a way to display God's presence and love and intervention! I believed it was a mission field for me to go to the hospital, for me to proclaim to doctors and nurses and other patients that Elliot's life was a testimony to God's miraculous intervention. Any time I thought the Holy Spirit was prompting me, I would share the story of the journey Elliot and I had been on. I would share the details of my dream, how God had already saved Elliot numerous times, and how he comforted me with Scripture, prayers of others, encouraging words, and especially my Promise. I felt so humbled and unworthy. So many other parents lost babies; why was I so blessed that God was going to keep mine alive? My faith grew and grew not because I believed I was going to get what I wanted but because I believed God was using our story to spread his name. My hope, my trust, my absolute faith was in God and what we all believed he had said.

The evidence before me continued to seemingly confirm that his hand was on Elliot. Doctors usually tell women whose water breaks early that they will go into labor within forty-eight hours. My water had already been broken for three weeks when I went into the hospital. I had already greatly beaten the odds. Then I continued to. I could tell the NICU doctor did not think it would be long before I'd have a baby. And, statistically speaking, it was reasonable of him to think so. But Elliot stayed put, and I stayed healthy for long past the gestation weeks anyone expected. My nurses and doctors were encouraged. Everyone talked about Elliot with expectancy in those later weeks, not with the hesitancy they had before. He'd grown to a safe gestation. And, while I knew lung development was the primary unknown in his health because of my lack of amniotic fluid, to me, this was just one more place for God to show up. God had shown up at every other point in this horrific pregnancy. How could I not trust that he who was knitting Elliot together in my womb could also knit his lungs?

The day of Elliot's birth, I went to sleep under that anesthesia, confident that my baby boy would be alive when I awoke.

And he was! Beautiful, big, precious Elliot William Treibel. There he was, a picture on my husband's phone, his perfect fingers wrapped around one of his daddy's.

The doctors were encouraged and amazed at Elliot's progress over the next few days. No one gave us any more serious talks about Elliot's "condition." The doctor who delivered him even smiled! The gratitude in my heart was impossible to describe. God was really doing it! Again and again, he was performing real-life miracles on behalf of *my* son! Those five days of Elliot's life outside the womb are possibly the most content, faith-filled days I've ever lived. Again, this was not because God was giving me what I wanted (though that was a bonus), but because God spoke to me, spoke through others, spoke through His Word, and was answering the prayers of hundreds of people. We were witnesses to His miracles.

Or so I thought.

Elliot had an up-and-down day on June 3. But even during the roller coaster, God seemed to be doing miraculous things.

So, the events from 5:30-6:00 p.m. on June 3 were impossible for me to understand, believe, or accept. Five months later, I still have moments where I think I'll wake up and this has all been one big, bad dream.

I returned from a brief nap, leaving Elliot in the capable hands of his nurse, who encouraged me to go rest. "You and Elliot both need some sleep." She was confident Elliot was fine. The doctor was confident. I was confident.

As I walked back to the NICU, I remember being so excited to spend the evening with my little guy now that I was a little more refreshed, and that I was finally feeling a little more recovered from my C-section. I stood at the sink washing my hands when a nurse walked briskly to me and said, "They have to replace Elliot's chest tube again." I nodded, and she led me to a chair at the nurses' station just outside his room. A medical team stood around him. This was a hard thing to watch, but I'd watched it twice before in the past five days, and whatever the problem was had been fixed. I talked to God. I prayed. I hated seeing my little guy struggle, but I did not for one second consider Elliot might die. I don't really remember much as I was sitting there. I remember texting updates to my husband. I remember hearing the oscillating ventilator. I remember starting to cry and someone saying, "Will someone go reassure that mom?" And someone did reassure me. Did they all still believe that Elliot would be fine?

The next thing I remember is the doctor coming out of Elliot's room and motioning for me to talk to him. I thought we'd discuss Elliot's present difficulties, and he'd give me an update or ask my permission to try some new intervention. So, it didn't quite register when he threw up his hands and only said, "It's not working!"

Okay. I breathed deeply. So whatever medical interventions they were trying were not enough. This made sense to me at that insane moment. God apparently wanted to show his glory through Elliot's little life, and what better way than showing this hospital staff a miracle?

I said, "Can I pray over him?"

The doctor nodded vigorously. "Sure!"

I still wonder, what did he think? Did he think I was praying over Elliot as a blessing before he died? Did the doctor hope prayer could heal him? Did he just want my son and me to be together?

I posted on Facebook for everyone to pray because the doctor thought we were losing Elliot. I couldn't wait to return with an update on the miracle of Elliot's return from the brink of death. Because Elliot *would. not. die.* God could not possibly have given that promise and confirmed it in so many ways and through so many people, saving him so consistently month after month, just to break his promise now!

I put my hands on my baby's head and little feet. A nurse next to me applied more pressure on my hands. Did she think that would heal Elliot? Or that my prayers would be heard more? Or was that for my benefit? All I could cry through my tears was, "Jesus, overcome. Jesus, overcome. Jesus, overcome."

As I prayed, friends, you must understand how convinced I was God would heal Elliot. Not. One. Doubt.

The rest of it is fuzzy. At some point, they said, "Do you want to do skin-to-skin?" Of course, I did! Maybe that's when he would be healed and start breathing. I think I saw a dramatization of something like that on a Facebook video once…

Suddenly there was a chair behind me, and I was sitting down, and Elliot was on me, and we were wrapped in warm blankets. Someone was manually pumping oxygen for him. It's all a blur. I don't remember when they stopped pumping his oxygen. I do remember them asking me how long it would take for my husband to get to the hospital. That was the first moment it clicked in my head that they were saying my baby was dying. Why else would it be urgent for Dustin to get to the hospital?

A nurse grabbed my phone and snapped pictures, the only pictures of me holding my son while he was still alive. At some moment, they said they were going to take out Elliot's tubes. Oh, how I wanted them to do something! I cried out, "Are you sure?!" I don't know what they said. The feeling of helplessness and horror is impossible to put into words.

I remember at some point, the doctor listening to Elliot's heartbeat with a stethoscope and saying, "Very faint."

And then, somewhere around 5:55 p.m., he put that stethoscope on Elliot's precious little back and said, "He's gone."

I have this picture in my mind of a mirror. It's a big mirror, perfectly crafted and polished. The mirror is my faith, and it was crafted by God throughout my whole life, but in the six months prior to this moment, it became clearer and more beautiful than it had ever been.

The moment Elliot died, God took a hammer to that mirror, to my faith, and slammed it into the perfect glass with unspeakable force. There are not even shards of glass lying on the floor; the mirror has been smashed to dust.

You might be able to imagine what it's like to have your child die in your arms. But unless it has happened to you, you cannot. Not really. I would've gladly died in his place or experienced even worse horrors and pain if only I could've saved him. There's no way to describe it.

And I immediately blamed God. I felt no "peace that passes understanding," as I've heard other bereaved parents describe. I pray that will come.

The doctor didn't know why Elliot died. All the interventions they'd been using for five days to keep him stable simply stopped working. Everyone was shocked. I couldn't say much to the doctor because, in the end, it was not his job to protect Elliot; it was God's.

I do not recognize this faith, the one full of doubts and anger. But God made the mirror. God annihilated the mirror. And only God can put it back together.

Since Elliot died, I have prayed little and read the Bible less. Sometimes I will read YouVersion's verse of the day because I think Elliot would want me to. But the only other thing I've read is the first few chapters of Job. This had always been a hard book to understand, and more so now. But there's one part of it that makes more sense to me than it ever has.

I remember a pastor once commenting on Job's unhelpful wife. Job had just lost all his livelihood, all his children, and now had nasty sores that tortured him. The advice of Job's wife? "Curse God and die!" Unfaithful, right? Probably.

But I've also heard before that the verbal venom people spew often comes from their own hurt. It dawned on me as I read this passage, *her children died!* All of them! Maybe "curse God and die" was how Job's wife felt. Does that seem over the top? Too dramatic?

I have cursed God.

I have wanted to die.

I am Job's wife.

I'm not saying it's right; I'm just saying it is.

Maybe Job's wife also felt abandoned and betrayed by the God she thought loved her. Maybe she even thought that she heard one thing from God and was delivered the exact opposite.

The frustrating reality is that if God is who I always believed him to be, then he really can't lie. He really can't be cruel for no reason. He really can't break a promise.

So that leaves it to me to take the fault. I heard wrong. I misrepresented God's intention. I used his Word to say something it wasn't meant to say. And these possibilities are just as scary as thinking God could lie or betray.

If I didn't hear him in this, and I so fully believed I did, then how will I ever know how to hear his voice again?

My future vision of my relationship with God stretches out before me in a weird sort of legalism: go to service, sing the songs, give some money, say the right words, and do good things. I guess I can do that. But how will my spirit ever soar again? I have no Elliot. I feel like Jesus is a stranger to me, and so I have no Jesus to counsel me through the loss of my baby. I have never felt more alone, more forsaken.

He made the mirror. He shattered the mirror.

If he's real, if he's love, if he's good, he will have to put the mirror back together. He alone must mend what he has broken.

I hope Job's wife found herself able to praise God again. I hope I will, too.

***

Can you believe it? Can you believe that we walked out of the hospital on a stupidly sunny June day without our beautiful son?

I still can't believe it.

I still can't believe it.

I don't believe a deeper pain exists than the pain of a parent's empty arms after a child dies.

The Threefold Insult

I didn't realize it then, but I was about to enter a season of utter despair in three areas. The first was trauma. I'd heard the terms "trauma" and "PTSD," and I'm sure I even joked after an intense event, "That was traumatic!" But I didn't really know what trauma and PTSD were. I was about to find out.

The second area was grief. I've heard grief described as "love with nowhere to go." There don't seem to be enough descriptors in the English language to explain the feelings after losing my child. "Sad," "bereft," "hopeless," or "disappointed" sound shoddy and inadequate. Grief is a counterpart to death, and death is the worst enemy I have ever known. The death of my little boy sentenced me to life without him, and grief is the never-ending weary cry of a mother who can't find her baby.

The third aspect of losing Elliot was losing God and losing my faith. Losing hope in everything I thought I knew about my Creator and my Savior. Any pious language or sentiments were ripped out of me. The religious comfort offered by others was acid on my wounds.

The me I had been, the girl who could hover among the stars with Jesus…she was gone.

Chapter Eight:
The Torment of Trauma

You have slain me, Lord. You have devastated and ruined me. I thought you'd promised Elliot's life, but this journey ended in his death. I don't know how to be confident in anything I think I hear from you anymore. —June 6, three days after Elliot's death

Clients who have suffered traumatic loss certainly present a more complicated therapeutic challenge, because both trauma issues and the underlying anguish of loss need to be addressed. Clients are often unable to fully touch the pain of their grief until the symptoms of trauma have lessened. And that often doesn't come until after the story of the trauma has been talked through many times in a safe therapeutic environment. The repetition of the story allows the brain to assimilate the images of the traumatic event. With familiarity, the brain's defense mechanisms trigger less and less. Life is no longer one continuous nightmare. —Patrick O'Malley, *Getting Grief Right*[2]

Living the Nightmare

Twenty hours. That's how long Dustin and I, along with friends and family, spent with our little boy's body before we had to say goodbye. You can't imagine it. I honestly can barely remember it. I think the traumatic shock of those hours has damaged my memory. But I do remember some things.

I remember how quickly after he died his limbs became stiff.

I remember how quickly his skin turned cold.

I remember needing to go to the bathroom hours after he died, winding through the hallways of the NICU, walking by all the rooms in which living babies breathed.

2 Patrick O'Malley and Tim Madigan, *Getting Grief Right: Finding Your Story of Love in the Sorrow of Loss* (Boulder, CO: Sounds True, Inc., 2017).

I remember my breasts becoming engorged and painful with milk for Elliot. For my son whom I would never nurse.

I remember the people who came. All our family members: my parents, Dustin's mom, our brothers and their wives, they were all suddenly around me, hugging me, weeping. I don't remember their words (for there are no words), but I will always remember their presence. And Jenny and Leslie, my dear college friends. How hard it must've been for them to see me and my dead baby. That was brave of them, kind of them. And Sandra, a friend who was a stranger then, arrived with her camera and took the most beautiful pictures, the ones I will share forever. She captured through a lens just how heaven-made Elliot was. I look back now and see that it was Christ for all those loved ones to enter that nightmare with us.

Well past midnight, I situated myself in the reclining chair in his NICU room, with Elliot wrapped in a soft blanket our family had brought to us. I couldn't fight fatigue any longer, so I settled into sleep with Elliot in my arms for a one-and-only night. I remember I dreamed it was all a bad dream, and that Elliot was okay. I shook awake and saw my dead little boy in my arms. There is nothing like the torment of knowing your worst nightmare has come true and you can never wake up. I remember despair swallowing me.

But mostly, I remember Elliot.

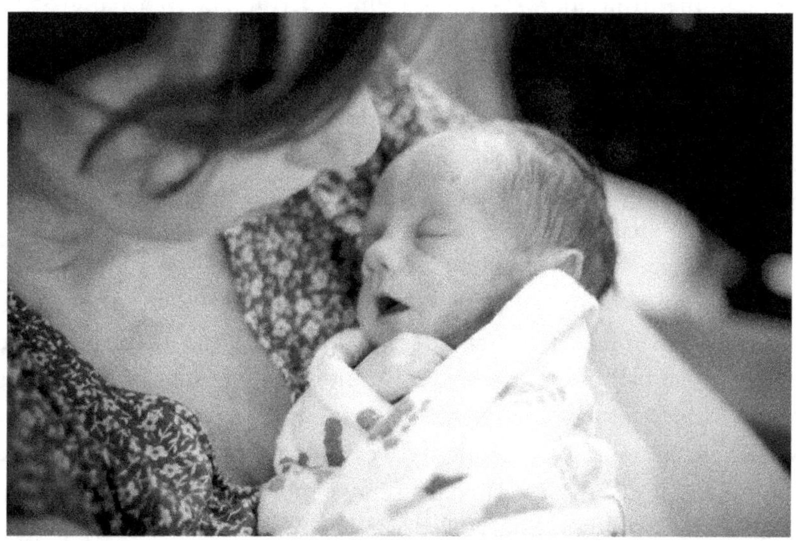

I remember how soft his hair was.

I remember how perfect his features were. You have never seen such a beautiful baby.

I remember how changed he looked the next morning. How the blood vessels around his mouth and under his nose were starting to break, so it looked like he was bleeding.

I knew it was time to let him go. So, without any choice in the matter, we left him there.

Walking through the front door of my home, eight weeks after Dustin had rushed me to the hospital, was surreal. The car seat I'd ordered for Elliot was in its box by the front door. Dustin had set up the crib in Elliot's room, there to be a pleasant surprise when I came home. The house was in disarray; just that week, new carpet had been installed, so Dustin had been moving furniture around to accommodate the installation crew. I remember how glad I was my baby boy would have soft new carpet to crawl and learn to walk on.

The second worst moment of my life, after the moment Elliot died, was telling his sisters that Elliot died. They stayed with Dustin's mom one day, then she brought them to us but had not told them about Elliot's death. We had never once told our girls there was a possibility Elliot would die because we truly did not consider it to be a possibility. I remember almost three-year-old Valerie bursting through the front door, shouting joyfully, "You had your baby!" She thought her little brother was alive. Pain upon pain upon pain.

We sat them down next to us. This was their first moment having their mommy home in two months, and instead of rejoicing, we were about to deliver a blow. I don't remember how we said it, but I think we just said it.

"Elliot died."

Oh, I can still hear Sylvia's wails. That sound burns through the years and pierces my mama's heart in the present. She had cried so tenderly and intensely when she was just three and I told her little Avery Rose had gone to heaven. But now, being older, a little more able to understand what pregnancy meant, what having a little brother would mean, and how constantly we assured her Elliot would come home, she was fully overjoyed to have another sibling. Now to rip it all away from her. She buried her head in my side and sobbed. I sobbed with her. I wanted to change this horrible reality. I wanted to make the world right again. I was so powerless.

The funeral came ten days after Elliot died. I guess that marks the third worst moment. People said the funeral was "beautiful," "meaningful," "honoring." I think, in the world of funerals, it was all those things. But again, I have very little memory of it. I remember Dustin and me spending time alone with Elliot before the funeral, and how different Elliot looked. I remember how cold he was. I remember how he felt in my arms, how he felt light and heavy at the same time. The last time I held him.

I walked around Little Ivy Chapel at Fairmount Cemetery before the service and placed framed photographs of Elliot all around the room. I remember some of the faces of people who came, and it was so meaningful that people took off work and traveled distances to be there. My brother Ryan played the piano. Gilbert, my second dad from Juárez, spoke. But I don't remember the music or what was said at the actual service. I just remember holding Sylvia while she cried. I remember opening the casket at the end so the girls and our families could see him and say goodbye.

I remember being the last one to touch him and kiss him before the casket was closed for good, and such a part of me died inside that my little light of a boy would not see light on this earth. I was enraged that we were going to bury him in the earth. Wrong, wrong, wrong. I remember it took everything in my power to drive away from the graveside and leave him there in that casket. I wanted to pluck him out and take him with me and scream to the earth, "You cannot have my baby, damn it!" I hate that day. I hate that moment. I find nothing beautiful in it.

And if only those awful moments were the end. But, as you may know, if you've lived through trauma, the actual traumatic moments are only the beginning. People grieve with you and feel so genuinely sorry for you. But no one can carry the trauma except the person who's endured it.

Dustin and I, along with our girls, our parents, our other extended family, and close friends, were embarking on a longer journey of recovery from this trauma as the rest of the world kept spinning.

And still, as those family and friends healed in their own times and ways, they kept moving in their own lives. So, Dustin and I remained behind, the only parents to this miracle boy who wouldn't grow up in our home.

And in a way, I remained behind Dustin. He could not know what it had been like to carry Elliot, to face the fear and hope and back again of the bleeding, the contractions, the feel of Elliot in my womb, the sound of his heartbeat those hours every day, the traumatic moment of being put under for my emergency C-section, Elliot dying in my arms.

My Little Bird

Trauma is so, so lonely. When compounded with the ache of grief for my child, the third child in a row I had buried, I fell into a pit that seemed to have no bottom.

And in that fall, I felt nothing from God. I felt nothing toward God. I woke each morning to a picture of Elliot on my wall and was sucked into a hole of horror I would have done anything to escape. But the only escape would be for reality to alter and Elliot to be alive. I knew it wasn't possible, but wildly, my mind wanted reality to change. So, despair became my constant companion. Lines from a poem by Gerard Manley Hopkins, my longtime favorite poet, hummed my theme:

> I wake and feel the fell of dark, not day.
> What hours, O what black hours we have spent
> This night! what sights you, heart, saw; ways you went!
> And more must, in yet longer light's delay.
>
> With witness I speak this. But where I say
> Hours I mean years, mean life. And my lament
> Is cries countless, cries like dead letters sent
> To dearest him that lives alas! away.
>
> —from "I Wake and Feel"[3]

---

3 Gerard Manley Hopkins, "Wake and Feel," Poetry Foundation (Poetry Foundation), accessed November 4, 2022, https://www.poetryfoundation.org/poems/44396/i-wake-and-feel-the-fell-of-dark-not-day.

I existed for my girls. They saved me, in a way, which is itself an ache in my heart because that should not have been their responsibility. I pulled myself out of bed for them, played with them the best I could, then needed a break to cry, which I'd do in the bathroom or in my closet. I played with them some more, put them in their room for nap time, then stole away to cry yet again. Dustin would get home, and we would cry. I paced the floor of my room in a strange panic and mumbled, "Where is my baby? Where is my baby? Where is my baby?"

The "comfort" of heaven was no comfort at all in those days. It felt like Elliot had been kidnapped, and by the God I trusted, no less. Heaven was hazy and uncertain, and the little body I carried in my womb was in the ground in a cemetery. What comfort was there in that?

My heart formed a song, the first song I had written in years. I wrote it for my boy about a month after he died.

> Away too soon. You gave me light.
> Where have you gone, my little bird?
> And why have you flown away?
> In my dreams you'll land and be with me.
> I'll cradle you and beg you to stay.
>
> But your wings have spread, my little bird.
> I'm left here on ground without you.
> I search the skies to catch a glimpse.
> But it's deep in my heart I've found you.
>
> To kiss your face. To hold your hand.
> So hard to wait, my little bird!
> If I could just touch you once more!
> How my arms ache to feel your warmth,
> But you've left earth's shackles to soar.
>
> Where have you gone, my little bird?
> And why have you flown away?
> In my dreams you'll land and be with me.
> I'll cradle you and beg you to stay.

Groceries & Validation

God, the phrase that keeps coming to my mind today is "rape of the soul." I don't know how to describe more graphically or accurately the damage and violation to my heart. To have trusted you so completely, to have given myself to your hands and entrusted you with my son, and to lose him so suddenly after so short a time…the most intimate parts of me have been torn apart. That's what it feels like. —July 26, one and a half months after

No one tells you how hard it is to buy groceries after the death of your child. That's not in any handbook.

It was just days after losing Elliot, before his funeral, I think. Dustin, the girls, and I were at a park near our house, and we needed something, though I can't remember what. I said I'd run to the Walmart Neighborhood Market up the road while Dustin stayed with the girls.

When I walked into the grocery store, I felt incapable of grocery shopping. I became sweaty and nervous for no apparent reason. The rhythm of my pulse drummed in my ears. The noises of shopping carts, scanners beeping, and people talking seemed to be magnified one thousand percent. The buzzing industrial lights overhead felt oppressive and oddly familiar. The hospital. They were like the lights in the hospital. And the people. The people! Just walking around like everything was fine in the world! What the hell were they doing just acting like life was normal? I couldn't breathe, couldn't think, couldn't keep it together.

I finished my shopping, though I likely did not get everything I intended, and made it back to my car to weep in hyperventilating sobs.

It was the first horrifying encounter with PTSD, but it would not be the last. Nor would I say I have emerged to a place where I don't have these episodes still occasionally. What an insult to injury. To lose a beloved child, then be haunted constantly by the physiological effects of trauma. Nothing made sense.

And my God, where was my God?

What was the purpose of all that faith you gave me to reassure of Elliot's

life? Like, really, what was the point? Because you either gave me that faith, that monumental faith that pushed away fear whenever it surfaced. Or you don't actually exist, in which case there is no hope for anything. Or I imagined everything I thought I heard from you, in which case, how can I ever trust again that I'm hearing from you? But if all that faith and hope and trust was really given to me by you to give me peace throughout all the scares, then why? Why did you take him anyway? Why did my worst fears come true? Why should I trust you again with anything? Why should I even believe you're there?

I believed you. I believed so completely. I feel betrayed by the one person I thought could never betray me. I don't know how to come back from this. If I have anything to offer you, this is it. My raw, aching, shredded heart. Because even though I don't know how to trust you anymore, I still know you are all there is when life is said and done. —August 14, two months after

Your Precious Little Pumpkin

Just a trip to the grocery store inflicted the wound of reminder that the world kept spinning without Elliot. The people who made a point to speak about Elliot, say his name, make a comment about his cuteness, all the friends and family and blog readers who validated him, these precious souls helped keep my mama's heart from drying up. Though I did not see God at all in those days, I now see how he showed up in people.

One of those people was Nancy, the trauma therapist Dustin and I began seeing about a month after Elliot's death. She had so much compassion, empathy, and wisdom. I trusted her because she talked about Elliot like a real person. Therefore, I could tell her everything. There was no belittling my pain, as if Elliot was "only a baby" (and yes, I have received that message, sadly).

I remember one session, I think I was minimizing my pain, wondering why I was hurting so badly. I'll never forget the way she said in her sweet voice, "Because you love your precious little pumpkin so much." Wow! It might seem like a small thing, but such a tender, silly, sweet way of referring to Elliot humanized him.

With Nancy's guidance, my brain slowly learned to create new pathways where trauma had broken them. As I told Elliot's story to her again and again, from different angles and out of various needs of my heart, I slowly was able to function. She often talked about "levels of distress." She showed a number line to Dustin and me, counting from 1 to 10, early on in our therapy sessions and asked where our distress levels fell on a regular basis regarding losing Elliot.

"I think a 4 most of the time, maybe a 6 or 7 when there's a trigger," Dustin replied.

I stared at the number line. "A 10," I said. "It's always a 10." It seemed absurd to me it could be anything else.

Nancy looked at me. "Well, we're going to work to bring that distress level down. It makes sense you will sometimes feel very distressed, but you can't live there all the time."

And though I couldn't have seen God's face in those days, I think he brought me comfort through Nancy. She validated every atom of my pain, and she also gave me tools to slowly emerge to the land of the living again.

Eclipse

I had been looking forward to the solar eclipse that August for five years, ever since I learned it would cross North America. Dustin and I became more intentional about doing fun things with our girls after Elliot died, I think both because we had a deeper appreciation for every moment with them and because we had to chase joy to keep from drowning in sorrow.

So, to find our way to Nebraska with my family to view the total solar eclipse was only natural, even though taking a trip so soon after his death took all our strength. We bustled out of our hotel room that morning to pursue a clear sky spot. It had been cloudy all morning, and we were worried we'd miss it. We wound through rural roads along with other eclipse chasers praying for a break in the clouds. Then, just in time, we found a perfect location with several other onlookers along a train track that ran parallel to an otherwise unknown Nebraska country highway.

The unseen moon inched slowly over the disc of the sun. Our eclipse-safe sunglasses ensured we could see just how perfectly the moon planned to overtake our solar ally. It was eerie to watch the sun being eaten away, to itself morph into a shape like a crescent moon. Yet, it stayed light until the moon completely won the battle. I'll never forget the moment of totality when the world around me turned to night, crickets chirped in the middle of the day, the temperature dropped suddenly, and all was haunting and beautiful. Stars burst forth. The stars, those friends whom so many times in life showed me God's face, reminded me the unseen is not unreal. The normally invisible corona of the sun shone a silent, radiant fire.

It was magic.

And then, two minutes later, daylight broke through once again. The August heat returned, the crickets silenced, and the stars hid from view once more. All the onlookers got in their cars and headed for home.

And something struck me as we drove away, the beauty of something yearned for and anticipated, so heart-achingly brief.

Elliot's life was so like the eclipse. So much anticipation and excitement for such a short few moments of indescribable beauty. Then it was over, only to be replayed in memory. Did the brevity of the eclipse make it less precious? No. More so.

So it is with Elliot. The brevity of his life is what makes the remembering it so, so precious. He shined so brilliantly. And so, he shines in my memory. — August 31, three months after

I was beginning an unfamiliar journey. It would take many months before the brain-altering effects of trauma could begin to settle enough for me to live moments without being in high distress constantly. Only once the PTSD, anxiety, and high alert lessened could I finally, truly begin to grieve. It would take many more months before I could unravel the anger, hurt, and disappointment enough to find space to want comfort from God, or even to believe he was there to offer it.

And in those long, torturous months, life was at a new level of lonely. People kept living, as was only natural. But inside, I had died with Elliot, and the me smiling at church or attending play dates was some pretender, some robotic version so, so empty.

Blog Post: "So This is Grief"

Three months after

So, this is grief.

Oh.

So, THIS is grief:

Watching the sky light up with the fire from dozens of hot air balloons. I smile as the giggles of my girls fill my ears. Then my eye catches the sight of the couple next to me swaddling their newborn baby on their picnic blanket. Elliot would be about that big now. Tears behind my eyes. Elliot should be here!

Or grief is being at library story time with my girls, when the lady next to me starts nursing her baby. What is she doing? Doesn't she know my baby is dead? Um, no. Of course, she doesn't. The world didn't stop when Elliot died. But grief sure thinks it should've.

So, this is grief:

Smiling as I look at Valerie sleeping in her car seat. I notice her perfect little mouth that looks just like Elliot's mouth, and picture how he would look so much like her, but with his dark hair. And my pulse races and my brain reels and my body panics that I will never, never, never see him asleep in his car seat.

So, this is grief:

Three months to the day from when that picture on the wall was taken, all those pictures of me holding Elliot as he sleeps. Forever sleeps. He really just looks like he's sleeping. Remembering with crystal clarity, and yet with almost no clear memory at all, the thirty-minute chaos of Elliot going from living to dying to died. And the *unbelievable* feeling of it all. Shock. Horror. Wishing, somehow, there was a miracle. A way to wake him up. Oh, come back to me, my baby!

Oh. So, this, THIS is grief. Shouting grief:

The song, the only song I can find that matches the intensity of my heart, and I turn it up in the car (or truck or van) and *scream* to get the pain out. Because the loss of my little boy deserves a really good scream now and then. Don't worry; I only scream when I'm alone. I'd love to know what the person in the car next to me thinks.

I see. This, too, is grief. Draining grief:

The fatigue precedes the grief, like a harbinger. My limbs become spaghetti, my thoughts become fuzzy, and I can't stop yawning.

Maybe I didn't sleep well. I should know better by now. My body's energy channels into my eyes, and they begin to spill hot tears as some particular memory plays out. I remember, I remember…his tiny little hand wrapped around my finger. The spot on my belly where his feet demanded my attention. The dances he did on the ultrasound screen. The tha-thump of his heartbeat. The doctor saying there was no heartbeat. I remember. And no energy returns to my body until I cry it out.

Oh, hello to this grief that finds me most days. Distracting grief:

I get the girls down for their nap as quickly as I can. That cookie dough ice cream in the freezer (people who bring ice cream are so nice) calls my name. I scoop out *way* more than the half-cup serving proposed, change into comfy pants to make room for the ice cream, and snuggle in front of the TV. I don't even like this Netflix show, but all I need is a distraction for forty-two minutes. I want to forget life, just for forty-two minutes.

Hmm. This one is interesting. Busy grief:

Do. Not. Get. In. My. Way. I am *cleaning,* darn it! Or organizing, or planning, or driving to and fro. Or rearranging furniture. Ah-ha. I think I'm feeling better. I feel so important with my many things to do. The busy likes to make me think the grief is on vacation.

This, most definitely, is grief. Guilty grief.

Why did I ever leave his side? Did he really know I loved him? *Why did I take that nap?* I did this. It's my fault. It was my broken body. I shouldn't have vacuumed that day. I shouldn't have let the ultrasound tech push so hard on my belly. Should not have picked up Valerie that other time. I should've kept my feet up more. Or less. I don't know!

Guilty grief is very loud. And no, saying, "It wasn't your fault," does not make the guilty grief go away. But thanks, anyway, for saying it.

Sometimes I run from the next grief, but I shouldn't. It takes a lot of energy, but it yields great rewards. Community grief:

It's the friend who comes over for a play date and looks at the scrapbook other friends made of Elliot's life. And she cries. Cries! With me and for me and for the loss of a baby that she, too, loved.

It's another friend who meets me at Elliot's grave and walks with me there, listening to all my impossible questions about God and not judging me for them.

It's my church family, who spends the Sunday morning after Elliot's death writing cards to my husband and me.

It's my friends who bring a meal. That act of service validates that our family is in something deep and crappy, and that it can be impossible to pull myself together long enough to make food. So, thank you for the meals.

It's the Facebook groups I am a part of where we cry it all out on the group newsfeed and say, "Amen to that. I understand."

And it's the dozens and dozens of stories written by other mommies who've lost babies, who feel like the only women in the world I have anything in common with right now.

It's my mother-in-law who hugs me hard every time she sees me because she just knows.

It's my friend who buys me coffee and asks about and listens to every detail of Elliot's death. She was brave enough to ask. And I so desperately needed to tell.

It's my dad, who puts a blue bird on his grave and writes letters and poems to Elliot.

It's my far-away friends who let me write and text the most random and sometimes disturbing thoughts from this horrendous journey.

It's my husband, who listens to me cry the exact same words over and over again. Who answers my irrational fear question, "We won't ever forget him, honey, will we?" with a comforting, "No, we will never forget him."

It's the friends who in a year or five years or ten years will still understand if I cry, who never expect me to "get over it," who will just be there to listen and love. These are the friends who will remain. I am blessed to have *many*.

This one is some serious grief. The hardest grief. The most confusing grief. The most comforting grief. The most angering grief. The most loving grief.

The God grief.

I am confident God can follow conversations that bounce around like pinballs. He'd have to, to keep up with a train of thought like this:

- What were you THINKING?!?!
- Why did he die?!?!?
- Oh, Lord, I am so, so sad. He's my son. Thank you for his life. He's the most beautiful gift you've ever given me. Some way, any way, use this loss in my life for your plan, bring beauty from these ashes…
- BUT WHAT HAPPENED?!?!? (Deep breath.)
- I know you see what I can't see, Jesus. I trust that in heaven we'll be reunited, and I'll understand. But for now, this is just STUPID!!!
- Seriously? Seriously? Are you even there, God? Forgive me, Lord. It's just so hard. MY BABY IS IN THE GROUND! THAT'S JUST DUMB! But he's at peace in you, isn't he, Lord? I trust he is….

And on and on it goes.

It helps. Some.

Then there is an unexpected grief. Beautiful grief:

I kneel at his grave, running the long grass through my fingers to touch anything that is close to him. There are those hot tears again, watering the grass, and I whisper a million things to my baby, to the body below and the soul above. I tell him his mommy is so proud of him. His sisters miss him so much. His daddy will never be the same. I tell him, "Your mommy is only so sad because I love you so much." I don't want him to think he did anything wrong. I grieve because I love him so much.

Grief.

Love.

Oh, wow.

Grief exists because of love. There is something beautiful in that.

So, this is grief. Three-month grief. It's different than it was at three days or three weeks or will be at three years. My nice counselor shows me a drawing of spirals, tightly wound together.

"You've heard of the stages of grief," she says. I mentally try to remember them…something like shock, anger, depression…but it ends with acceptance, right? She goes on.

"What you may not have heard is that your brain circles through the stages of grief over and over again."

I gulp. That doesn't sound like fun.

But she explains as she draws the tight little spirals. "Right now, you are experiencing the stages of grief one on top of another." Then she slows her hand and spreads out the spirals, making each circle bigger. "Eventually, you will experience those stages, those waves of grief, more spread out and with less intensity. But the grief will always be there in some form."

Grief will always be here. Hmm. It does make sense. Because love will always be here.

So, this, all this, is my grief. It somehow must be a part of me, and yet not all of me. It can't be pushed away and ignored, and it can't rule forever. I think God can use it to be a friend, but the enemy wants to hijack it, to dismantle me, make me unrecognizable.

I don't think Elliot would want that. I think he would want God to use it to make his mommy beautiful. Sometimes very sad, other times very angry, but beautiful in God's sight.

This is grief on September 3. A night of remembering. Of missing him. But mostly, I hope, of love.

Chapter Nine: Blame

Weeping in the Parking Lot

On Elliot's three-month birthday, I found myself back at the weekday Bible study I'd attended the previous two years. Though I sought comfort there, it was awful. I couldn't understand why I hated it so much. I'm sure part of it was trying to force myself to do a Bible study when I wasn't sure I believed in the Bible anymore. All I could do was show up with a blank workbook and somehow make it through the class without talking or crying. Or rolling my eyes at the lady who hugged me in the hall and said, "We just don't understand God's will. You'll have another one."

Or maybe it was pointed comments in prayers during the small group: "Lord, we don't understand why some in this group have gone through such hard things, but we trust your plan for our lives and that you have everything in your control."

Maybe it was after I politely smiled at one lady who made a point to comment on my "returning smile" as if I was therefore "over it."

Or could it have been that, even though I told the story of Elliot's life and death at the beginning of our semester, a lady had to ask again a few months later, "So, was your son actually…born?"

I felt as invisible as my son.

The dread and discomfort worsened as the year went on. My attendance was purely for my girls, so they could have their once-a-week little class with crafts and songs. I would hold it together during my small group sessions, then flee to my car during the large group sessions when I knew no one would notice my absence. Every week, my silent car would listen to me cry because I felt so unseen, unknown, trapped in the expectation of moving forward, moving on.

People didn't know they were doing it, but in their attempts to make God so much bigger than the death of my son, they weren't making God bigger for me. They were making my son seem smaller. Their assurance of God's plan and his will was only serving to infuriate me more, reinforcing the damning proclamation that Elliot's death was from him, a decision God made.

Screaming Song

And since God seemingly made this decision, a myth perpetuated by Christians around me, I was so, so angry at him. I visited Elliot at the cemetery every week, sometimes twice a week, for several months after he died. I could not help but scream at God every time I drove there. Once, I had Mumford and Sons playing, and the song "White Blank Page" came on as I turned into the cemetery. I doubt the songwriter had my scenario in mind, but the words fit so well that it became a screaming theme song for many more trips to the cemetery.

> Tell me now, where was my fault
> In loving you with my whole heart?
> A white blank page and a swelling rage
> Rage
> You did not think when you sent me to the brink
> To the brink
> You desired my attention but denied my affections
> My affections
> So tell me now where was my fault
> In loving you with my whole heart?[4]

Oh, a good scream is what I needed many days. The ending of that song became a cynical prayer, with a hurt and broken child underneath the cynicism.

> Lead me to the truth and I
> Will follow you with my whole life

I kept wanting God to appear in some big, undeniable way. But he didn't, and truthfully, I don't think I would have accepted it if he did. If he had brought me a miracle to show he was with me, I would have

4 Mumford & Sons. "White Blank Page." *Sigh No More*. Markus Dravs, 2008.

screamed and thrown it back in his face.

"You are too late!" I would've spewed at him. I had the words ready. "You should've used your miracles to save Elliot!"

So, he came in quiet ways: in conversations, in songs, and in books. He came in ways I would not have recognized it was him.

God's "Plan"

A kind friend gave me the book *Is God to Blame?* by Greg Boyd a few months after Elliot died. I didn't know what I'd find in its pages. The title succinctly described my thoughts, though. And the impression I got from church leaders, Bible study ladies, and the guy on the Christian radio station was that I would not like the answer to that question. No one would want to put "blame" on God, but it came back to that cliché "p" word: PLAN.

God's plan, they'd say.

God's plan cannot be thwarted.

God's plan cannot be undone. Interchangeable with God's "will," God's plan is the one that succeeds, and we believers need to come to terms with that.

If it happened to you, it was God's will. It was God's plan.

It is this very concept that I now believe was at the core of why Elliot's death devastated my faith so much and why I could not find any comfort in God. How could the one who planned to take Elliot's life comfort me in Elliot's death? Especially when Elliot had been rescued from death so many times in my womb, and I had been certain God was miraculously protecting him? When I believed God sent me a dream that promised the life of my son? How could I find comfort in any of this?

When I read *Is God to Blame?* though, a light cracked through my darkness for the first time since losing my baby boy.

Boyd postulates in his book that God's will is not always done, and Jesus is proof. Jesus' light came to fight against the darkness that sometimes does have temporary victory. Jesus proclaimed this world under Satan's rule, and whether Satan is literal or figurative is beside the point. Jesus liberated the sick and demon-possessed and indicated their trials were the opposite of what God wanted for their lives, not that these oppressions were God's will. He came to restore, not raze our fragile human race. Boyd calls this the "warfare worldview" in which we are aligned with the winning side of a war that continues to rage. A war in which good and evil, perfection and fallenness, health and sickness, are at odds with one another. Sometimes evil wins a battle. But Christ will win and has won the war.

Near the end of Boyd's book, a quote caused tears to flow in a beginning waterfall of relief.

> We are in a war zone, and everything hangs on our being able to identify who is fighting against us and who is fighting for us. The ultimate criteria for deciding what is and is not from God is Jesus Christ. If the one who died on the cross wouldn't have done it, you have every reason to assume an event is not from God or part of his will. Living with this Christ-centered perspective, we are freed from asking the unanswerable question of why life unfolds the particular way it does, and we are empowered to do something about it.[5]

Why had no one said this to me? Maybe a few people had, but I was still too encased in a previous viewpoint to hear them. I pictured Jesus, the real Jesus who healed children, and I couldn't see my Savior willing the death of such a paragon of beauty as my Elliot. I couldn't envision this Jesus willingly afflicting my already broken mama's heart with more brokenness. If this was true, if in his loving sovereignty, God did not "cause" the death of my son but rather hated it, I could maybe, *maybe* approach him again.

It was the beginning of a slow emergence back into some light. Though I had no framework to understand what things God willed, which things God allowed, and which things just plain happened, I was finally given a way out of the hell I lived in. And yet, finding my way out would prove to be a lonely road in its own way. The assumptions about God's will which had defined my old framework were still the assumptions held by most of my friends and church family. But I couldn't return to that viewpoint. I could not return to who I was before Elliot forever changed me.

---

5 Gregory A. Boyd, *Is God to Blame?: Moving beyond Pat Answers to the Problem of Suffering* (Readhowyouwant.com Ltd, 2011).

Working It Out in Writing

My thoughts toward God continued to be so dark, so intertwined with anger, self-blame, God-blame, and desperation to have my little boy back. So, I wrote. I wrestled in my writing because I could not force my friends and family to listen to my replaying record day after day.

I feel like I just survive each day, waiting to get each day over with. I don't feel like I'm really living…Please tell me this is not your "will" or your "plan." I think I can eventually accept you allowed this horrible attack of Satan because you could foresee bringing beauty from ashes. But how can I accept that you intentionally brought forth Elliot, just to fulfill your "plan" to kill him five days later? —September 19, three months after

Rebuild this shattered heart one shard at a time. You will have to tell me what my faith in you is supposed to look like. No one else can really tell me. And I feel very resistant to people trying to tell me. —September 27, three and a half months after

I hope someday my heart is healed enough to truly love adopted children. They've never been second-best to me. —October 4, four months after

I don't know how hope for heaven can carry me through a lifetime of missing him. —October 6, four months after

Conversations and a book I'm reading have helped me face the question of: where is God in all this? I feel a big relief that I might not have to blame God after all. Then do I blame Satan? Or my sin? Or the fallen world? —December 8, six months after

I almost don't want this year to end, because it will take me further and further from my short time with him. Every part of this journey hurts, all of it makes me ache. But I realize I've relived his death repeatedly so that it's just a well-etched memory in my brain. Making his scrapbook and looking at every picture taken of him while he was alive has helped me inhabit those five days, almost to imagine I'm back there, amid bliss. The long hospital wait over, my son born, everything worth it because I could see him, touch him, change his diaper, feed him milk. God, what I wouldn't give to have a story of a long NICU journey that ended with him coming home. I just want to live in those five days and never leave. —January 1, seven months after

I laid bare my honest soul before God and myself. I see now there was nowhere to hide these painful groanings, so I just kept letting them flow. And when I found a message in my written thoughts that felt universal, I refined and edited it into a blog post. Though my blog posts have never gone viral or changed the world, I've received enough comments and messages to know these struggles are real for many people, not just me. Somehow, processing my trauma through words has given voice to the pain others bear but don't know how to articulate.

I know the value of that gift because that's exactly what the writers of other blogs, books, and poems have done for me. Sometimes you need another voice to explain to your heart just what's going on. Words poured out from another soul into your own can be reminders to take courage. Other voices can remind us to believe beyond all reason that the loneliness is a liar and that you and I are not alone and never will be.

Blog Post: "The Big 'But'"

Seven months after

I've been staring at this picture a lot recently. It's one of my favorite pictures of Elliot. But let's be honest. They're all my favorites. When pictures of your child are finite, and when there will be no more, they are sacred. Dustin texted me this picture the day after Elliot was born while I was receiving my blood transfusion. It was the first time I saw him in his cool shades. I love how my little boy is snuggled up to his daddy's hand and how his expression looks like he's smiling. He looks so calm, so peaceful. I notice the way his index finger is curled over his thumb on his right hand. So perfect. Just a baby being a baby. I cherish it, like I cherish every image of my son.

The emotions rolled into an experience, like looking at this picture, are hard to describe, but maybe you are feeling them too. It is hard to look at pictures of Elliot, knowing I will never compare his growing form to his newborn pictures. There will only ever be newborn pictures. My soul recoils in anguish at this thought, so I cry. But then I see his perfect little features, his precious cheeks, his smooth skin, his fuzzy hair, his chicken legs…and I smile. I laugh. I tell him over and over that he is so stinkin' cute Mommy can hardly stand it! These reactions happen in me simultaneously. Just looking at a picture brings a whirlwind of emotions.

Prior to Elliot's death, I've been apt to downplay negative emotions with a big "BUT." I think this comes from a good place within myself and many Christians when we want to remember the bigger picture of God's love and his ultimate plan for our redemption in eternity. We don't want to get so caught up in any earthly trial that we focus only on temporary suffering. Phrases like, "This is a really hard time, BUT God is good," or "I'm really struggling, BUT with God's help, I'll get through it," are designed to refocus our perspectives. That's not a bad thing.

However, I've noticed that the big "but" often has an undesirable side effect: the minimizing of suffering. Nothing soothes a suffering heart quite like being validated; nothing adds a layer of hurt quite like being minimized. I know I am not the only mom of a deceased baby who has received phrases meant to comfort but accomplish just the opposite. Phrases like, "It's so sad you lost this baby, BUT you can have another one" (which is not true for me and many bereaved moms), or "I know you miss your son, BUT at least you have your girls." An English teacher like me tends to focus on semantics. The conjunction "but" in phrases like those has the effect of minimizing the first half of the sentence and maximizing the second. Hearing these phrases feels like being told to look on the bright side. But that's the thing about my child dying: there is no bright side.

In many other circumstances, it has been helpful to seek a silver lining. Any other problem I've encountered in my life, be it health issues or financial instability or relational conflict or a job I hate or severe depression, has had at least the possibility of improvement. With an awful job, though it can make one feel stuck and hopeless, there is at least a chance for a different job at some point in time. I have been in a pit of depression before and have felt very alone there. Yet even in that dark place, there has been the slightest glimmer of hope that it will not last forever.

Not so with the death of a child. The moment the doctor uttered those reality-altering words, "He's gone," I knew. I knew the horrifying reality those words represented. My very first thought was, "My son can never, never, never be alive again!" Other bereaved parents understand how that moment changes you at the core. The death of my child has no bright side, no possibility of change, no "but." At least not in this life. Without the hope of resurrection and eternity with Jesus, there would really be no point in anything. Yet, for the rest of this life, the fact of Elliot's death can never improve.

But (it's still a conjunction that serves a purpose), there is more. This world of conflicting emotions has led me to think not in terms of "either/or," but "both/and." I'm not happy or sad. I'm happy *and* sad. I'm not depressed or hopeful. I'm depressed *and* hopeful. For me, phrases now sound more like: "I'm devastated my son died, *and* I am so thankful I have my girls." Having two beautiful daughters does not assuage the pain of Elliot's death. Elliot's death does not diminish the joy of having my daughters. Pain and joy exist simultaneously.

My husband and I have started calling missing Elliot our "background noise." Our ache for Elliot is always, always, always present. Sometimes we get rightfully caught up in the fun of family and life, and we laugh until our sides hurt. In those times, the background noise is within our awareness but not at the forefront. Other times, when there is some time to reflect and remember, or when a trigger appears in daily life, the background noise is loud and needs to be acknowledged.

Just today, we took the girls to the museum with some friends. On the way to the museum, we drove past the cemetery and along the route that leads to St. Joseph's Hospital. This increased the volume of my background noise as memories of the hospital flooded my brain. Later, when the girls were playing in one of the crazy kid areas, I saw a precious baby boy, probably around seven months old, giggling and smiling at his daddy. He reminded me so much of how I picture Elliot would look and act now, and suddenly the background noise became the only thing in my awareness. I had to excuse myself to the bathroom and cry. And then, I enjoyed the rest of the morning with my bright-eyed little girls.

Early on after Elliot's death, several veteran bereaved parents lovingly warned me that I would never "get over it," and that only a "new normal" would help me put one foot in front of the other for the duration of my earthly life. I am realizing that this new normal is what I'm experiencing: the *and* of every moment. I'm playing with the girls, *and* I miss Elliot. I'm eating chocolate, *and* I miss Elliot. I'm singing, *and* I miss Elliot. I miss Elliot, *and* I think about adoption. I miss Elliot, *and* I'd like to plan a mission trip to Juarez. I miss Elliot, *and* I want to honor his life by loving others well.

I recall lines from "When I Survey the Wondrous Cross" that remind me of these thoughts.

> See from his head, his hands, his feet
> Sorrow *and* love flow mingled down
> Did e'er such love *and* sorrow meet?
> Or thorns compose so rich a crown?[6]

It's not that there was a lot of sorrow, *but* love erased it. It's not that there was abundant love, *but* sorrow killed it.

Sorrow and love. Joy and pain. Hope and despair.

I can't exclude any aspect of these conflicting emotions with a big "but." Perhaps accepting my background noise is one of the ways to continue moving forward. It's the only way I can picture moving forward at all: with love and longing for Elliot present continually. Though remembering him always brings pain, as looking at pictures does, it also brings hope and love and light and joy.

And one day in the future, when all is set right, I will finally be able to say, "I have missed you, my baby boy. But…we are together again."

---

6 Watts, Isaac. Communion Songs. "When I Survey the Wondrous Cross." *1902 Hymnals*, n.d.

Chapter Ten:
I Will Fight

This is the darkness of faith: when you've had to drop the old for a time but haven't yet found the new. It's the terrible space in between, where nobody wants to live. We want to retreat to a spot where I know who I am and who God is—even when our self-image and our image of God destroy each other, which often happens. —Richard Rohr, *Falling Upward*[7]

As people who reflect on suffering in the light of the cross, and as people who know God as he has been decisively revealed in Christ, we have no reason to assume there is a particular divine reason behind every instance of suffering we confront…We ordinarily can't know why particular individuals suffer the way they do. But in the light of God's revelation in Christ, our assumption should be that their suffering is something we should oppose in the name of God rather than accepting it as coming from God. Hence the only relevant question disciples of Jesus should consider is, What can we do to bring God's redemptive will into the situation, to alleviate suffering and glorify God? —Greg Boyd, *Is God to Blame?*[8]

The Dark Secret

Here is the crux of something dark and difficult to talk about.

My misuse and misunderstanding of God's supposed promise to me may have contributed to Elliot's death. If I had truly understood that his life dangled by a precarious thread, I may have done things differently. If I'd known how crucial those tiny amounts of fluid were to his lung development, I may have demanded my legs and hips

7 Richard Rohr, *Falling Upward: A Spirituality for the Two Halves of Life* (La Vergne: SPCK, 2013).

8 Gregory A. Boyd, *Is God to Blame?: Moving beyond Pat Answers to the Problem of Suffering* (Readhowyouwant.com Ltd, 2011), p. 84.

be elevated 24/7 while I survived on a catheter, bedpan, and sponge baths. I don't know if that would have saved Elliot. But I know I'll always be haunted by the fact that I didn't try.

I didn't try because the doctors told me "bed rest" included walking a bit, going to the bathroom, taking showers, and standing from time to time. They told me this was healthy for Elliot and me. Elliot kept producing urine that was supposed to become his amniotic fluid. He had working kidneys that made plenty of what he needed. But because my amniotic sac had ruptured, it had no way of staying inside my body except if I had used gravity to keep it forced inside. But instead, I followed the doctors' advice and moved. And every time I did so, Elliot's precious fluid of life gushed out of me onto a waiting industrial-sized maxi pad. How many pads did I throw away into that hospital bathroom trashcan which contained the substance my son desperately needed to survive?

But more than what the doctors told me was what God had told me. I didn't try to remain motionless and elevated for fifty days because God had given me a promise. I was as careful as the doctors recommended, but no more than that. I thought that since God had promised Elliot's life, nothing could undo that promise, even a lack of amniotic fluid.

I had a high level of trust in God, my interpretation of dreams and songs and Bible passages, and the prophetic proclamations of others. This trust may have been destructive to my child.

This kind of faith, it seems, can be a danger. It can undo reason and medical evidence. It can silence valid worry and create a false narrative in which faith equals the absence of doubt.

And this may have killed my son.

I don't know if this is the case, and I'll never know. I just know I really will never forgive myself for putting my faith above my son's wellbeing.

When Do We Pray Like This?

It was unnerving to emerge from the initial months of grief and trauma, to poke my head up and peer around, and realize that the world looked completely different.

Sundays were the worst. My church family had been nothing but kind and loving toward us. The morning after he died was a Sunday, and they spent the time after church writing cards to our family, which showed up at our door, and I will cherish those notes forever. The people there loved us the best people can love. They did what I would have done.

The person I couldn't find at church was God. It wasn't that the songs or sermons were any different than they would have been before Elliot died. It was that those lyrics and preaching were now fingernails on a chalkboard. The place I was supposed to go to connect with God was ripping me further from him.

One morning, when I was already reluctant to be there, the topic of the sermon was prayer. I don't remember exactly what was said, but I remember my friend who shared the sermon becoming passionate as he spoke. He recounted a biblical hero's intensity of prayer, how this hero believed God would answer, how this hero would not rest until God had performed a miracle, the great faith this hero possessed. Then he cried out in preacher voice, "When do *we* pray like this?"

I suppose it was meant to convict the hearer. But it did not convict me. It enraged me. I stood up and went to the bathroom, knowing I could not remain.

The words rolled around me as my most traumatic memory replayed over and over. "Can I pray for him?" I'd asked the doctor. My hands on Elliot's head and feet in his incubator, praying through tears, "Jesus, overcome! Jesus, overcome!" Knowing, believing, and full of faith that God heard me, and that God would act.

When do we pray like this? When had I prayed like this? The moment it mattered most. Without doubt, without a shred of uncertainty, I had prayed like this. And what had occurred instead of an answer to my prayer? My beautiful son's heart stopped beating! You bet I had prayed like this. How dare he insinuate in a blanket statement in a generalized sermon that I had not prayed like this! I took it so personally.

Some friends found me crying. Such good friends. Looking back, I was not as alone as I felt. They surrounded me and cried with me. They didn't need to ask why I was upset.

Tiny Growth

It's been almost six months since I last saw and held my sweet baby boy, and I still wake every morning with a sick feeling in the pit of my stomach and disbelief in my mind. My baby died. How did this happen? Please let it be a bad dream. Please bring him back somehow. My baby died. My baby died. Waking up is so awful.

I feel so isolated. With friends. With family. At church. I know how I should act, and usually, I can act that way. I should listen to other people. I should be friendly. I should find other things to talk about than Elliot or the pain of losing him. It's been a while. Kind people, close friends—they will still ask. They will let me talk. But even then, I can't go on and on. I have to be a little bit socially normal.

But what they can't see is how badly I want to crawl into his grave and forever sleep with him. They can't see it. I don't think they'd understand. I mean, what would they even say?

So, I pretend. I pretend. I pretend. And I am so, so lonely. —November 20, six months after

I feel like I'm trying to reach out to you, God, and probably you're sending comfort in ways I don't realize, but I don't hear you, don't feel you, and don't know if you're there. I just see Elliot—his little mitt-covered hands clutching my fingers, the only time I saw his precious, blinking eyes. And now it's like he was saying goodbye. Or was he calling for help? Oh, please show me he's okay and I'll see him again! This is killing me. —December 22, seven months after

As half a year went by, I felt no further in my grief journey or faith journey than the day Elliot died. Just six weeks after giving birth to Elliot, I went to the doctor's office for my routine post-delivery examination. The unsuspecting nurse who examined me had no idea the baby I'd delivered a month and a half earlier had died. When she came to do her exam, I began weeping uncontrollably. She called for a therapist to come to talk with me. They neatly labeled my paperwork, "grief reaction." The therapist listened as I briefly recounted my journey with Elliot. Her attempt at encouragement would later produce a cynical chuckle in me.

"It's normal for you to feel and react this way. This just happened. I mean, if you're still feeling and reacting this way in, say, six months, then that wouldn't be normal."

On Elliot's six-month birthday, I got his footprint tattooed on my foot. And I remembered the conversation with that doctor's office therapist with irony. I was anything but "normal" by her definition, as I had similar "grief reactions" every single day.

But I think now there was movement on my mixed-up, crazy path. Almost daily, I cycled through the grief of missing him, the trauma of his death, the desperation for God, the self-blame, the anger toward God, and the determination to live again. It felt like I was getting nowhere.

But looking back now, I think every time I came back around, I was a little stronger, a little more certain of what I was leaving behind and for whom I was pressing forward. I became a little more confident in questioning conventional wisdom, as I'd done as that college student not so sure musical instruments were of the devil. I became a little more hopeful, like that twenty-something who sat in a room in Juárez certain of Jesus's personal presence. I became a little less certain the mainstream was the right stream, like that new mom who listened to sermons on hell and was changed.

My growth was so tiny that I didn't feel it. Does a tree feel its growth?

I really do wish I had Jesus back. That I felt like I knew him, could talk to him and could trust him. I wish I could have the relationship with him that I thought I had before. Now, I feel like I'm talking to empty air. How do I really know he's there and that he hears me and that he cares? I know, I know. Faith. But I had faith that Elliot would not die nine months ago, that Jesus could answer my prayers and save my little boy's life. I had faith. And yet…here I am, nine months later, with empty arms and a pretty headstone on a changeless grave. —March 3, nine months after

I was unable to recognize the reality that all the words, feelings, thoughts, wrestling—these things *were* the growth. A very wise friend who I'd later go to for more help reminded me of something. I told her how hard church was for me, how I felt so resistant to feeling God. She didn't think that was a bad thing. She said, "You only resist something that's really there."

So, I slowly kept fighting as the first year after my son's death rolled by. It was a surreal year. Every single day, I retreated into a hollow space, a grief space, where I had to cry and remember and mourn. Life was so abnormal. I wondered if this was how life would always be. I felt weary, and at the same time determined. Elliot's life counted for something! I would not, *could not*, give up and let it all be for naught.

Blog Post: "Poor in Spirit"

Eight months after

A long time ago, a guy who loved Jesus named St. John of the Cross wrote a poem called "The Dark Night of the Soul." I don't know much about St. John, and I'm not crazy about the poem, but several months ago, my counselor sent me an email article with this quote:

"The Dark Night of the Soul, as John conceived it, is actually an inner state that may or may not have anything to do with external circumstances. It is an experience of being stripped of all the spiritual feelings and concepts with which we are accustomed to propping up our inner lives. It is a plunge into the abyss of radical unknowingness. This spiritual crisis, John assures us, is a cause for celebration because it is only when we get out of our own way that God can take over and fill us with love. But it's a grueling process to come to this level of surrender, and few of us go willingly."[9]

She sent me this article, I think, because she recognized in me the theme of what this "Dark Night" represents. The phrase in that quote, "an experience of being stripped of all the spiritual feelings and concepts with which we are accustomed to propping up our inner lives," just slammed me in the face. *That's it*, I thought, *the whole infrastructure of who I thought God was, and what I believed about Him, has all come crashing down*. You see, I'd built in my mind how God did things, how I related to him, and how he related to me. I didn't know I'd done that, but we probably all do it to some extent. I think it

9 Mirabaii Starr, "Dark Night of the Soul," *Wordpress*, January 7, 2010.

must be a necessary kind of reaction to the incomprehensibility of the infinite: we have to cushion ourselves with some religion.

The death of a child understandably causes a crisis of faith in many people, but I've noticed not in all people. Many bereaved parents I know personally or know of through their writing have felt all the emotions that accompany grief, along with feeling angry toward or abandoned by God. But some also felt Jesus' presence in the room with their dying child or proclaimed Job's "the Lord giveth and the Lord taketh away," or experienced peace that passes understanding in the darkest moment of their lives (Job 1:21 KJV). I've heard parents say as simply a matter of fact about their child-loss journey, "I was never angry with God." These people have inspired me to know that faith can survive hellish nightmares. I think these people may be stronger than me, or perhaps their original faith was "propped up" with more durable materials than mine.

But we're all different. I admire those people, but I am not like them in this facet of the grief journey. For me, my faith was knocked over, stripped bare, and swept away in a tidal wave of disbelief, disappointment, and rage.

So, what was left?

Do you remember the best of all '80s movies, *The Neverending Story*? Shame on you if the answer is no. At the end, when "The Nothing" has swept away the land of Fantasia, the Empress (yes, I've seen this movie too many times) remains with Bastian in the dark and she opens her hand to show him one glowing grain of sand. "This is all that's left of Fantasia," she tells him. But the good news, she says, is that when Bastian makes wishes on this tiny grain of sand, Fantasia can return and become more beautiful than ever.

My inner life, my spiritual walk with the Lord, was not just "propped up" before Elliot died. It was beautifully built and ornate, a land of beauty with spires and towers and clear streams and stunning skies. I had never felt such a sense of God's personal closeness to me: his care, involvement, plan, and power. Even the very moment I awoke from my short nap to return to Elliot's NICU room, I remember peace permeating every pore of my being. It was as if Satan waited for the moment when I was the most beautiful to disfigure me.

Because then I walked down that corridor, full of life and

anticipation and hope, and the clearest, purest faith I've ever felt. They said they were working on Elliot. And I did not fear; I believed. And then I saw his numbers drop. And still I did not fear; I believed. And then the doctor said there was nothing they could do. *Still*, I didn't fear. I held on to belief in what I thought God had said. And then I laid my hands on my son and prayed in Jesus' name for God to heal him, completely convinced God would do just that.

And then he died.

And just like that, the things that had held up that pristine, innocent faith, just collapsed. I feel like I don't have adequate words to describe it. My baby was gone. My world was gone. My faith was gone.

Or was it?

There's been a discovery of my own grain of sand, and it started off subtly. It began one day in September when I was texting a friend who was graciously checking in on me. I tried unsuccessfully (because it's texting) to share my heart. Her response was not quite what I wanted or thought I needed. This is no criticism of my friends; I believe I have quite possibly the most perfect mix of friends anyone could ask for. But I realized that no matter what my friends said, how they loved me, or what they did for me, it would never be enough. I needed a friend who could be with me constantly, caring for me relentlessly, and listening to me endlessly.

Oh. No human being exists who can fill that role…

Ah, I thought upward, *it's you, isn't it, Jesus?*

So that was the day I knew I had to allow him in again. I wasn't going to survive this nightmare alone.

But…how did I do it now? You know, how would I do the stuff Christians are supposed to do when my own Fantasia had been demolished? All the inner workings of how I did spiritual things had been knocked over. Phrases like "soak in the Lord" and "press into prayer" and "spend time in the Word" felt vague and untouchable. The questions in my Bible study book seemed to be written in gibberish. When I attempted to sing along at church, my throat would close up. Closing my eyes to pray was pretense.

My routine for years had been to sit with my Bible and my journal and alternate between what I was reading or studying in the Bible with talking to Jesus through my prayer journal. It was a process I enjoyed and helped me to grow in the knowledge and love of the Lord.

Now, however, sitting with my journal and Bible simply felt like two stacks of paper laughing at me. I couldn't hear God much from the pages of my Bible. I couldn't say much to him in the pages of my journal. Really, it was kind of like coming face to face with "The Nothing." I was bereft of God, encapsulated in my own dark night of the soul.

After twenty-one years of being a follower of Jesus, really? There was nothing? I felt a little like Paul in 2 Corinthians 11, when he makes a point by boasting of his religious deeds. It felt a little crazy that, after all the times I've read the Bible cover to cover, all the in-depth Bible study and Bible memorization, Christian college, mission work, the worship songs I've written, the short stories I've created about biblical characters, the conversations with Jesus, the conversations with others about Jesus…with all these experiences in my history, I was now at a complete loss.

I tried to read and study the Bible like I used to and got nothing.

I tried to write in my prayer journal, but I had nothing.

I tried to play my guitar and sing, but there was nothing.

It was as if my spiritual eyes had gone blind. Finally, I was ready to be comforted by the Lord and seek him in the darkest days of my life, and all my religious "go-to"s were coming up completely empty.

One day in November, I think, I just sat on the floor of my closet and cried out to him, "I have nothing to bring you! Nothing to say! Nothing to pray! I have *nothing*!" I realized that my spirit was just so, so bereft of, well, anything. The word "poverty" came to mind. I felt so, so poor inside.

Poor in spirit.

That famous phrase from Jesus' sermon on the mount stuck out in my mind. Is this what it could mean? Probably not coincidentally, I had begun reading all the red words in the gospels (a.k.a., the words of Christ). An overabundance of opinions and interpretations of the Bible exist, and I felt like I needed to rediscover what Jesus has to say. So, there I was, reading some of his very first recorded words:

"Blessed are the poor in spirit, for theirs is the kingdom of heaven" (Matthew 5:3).

Jesus' next statement broke me.

"Blessed are those who mourn, for they shall be comforted" (Matthew 5:4).

For the first time, my little grain of sand lit up. For the first time since Elliot died, I felt like Jesus was near.

Blessed are the poor in spirit, for theirs is the kingdom of heaven. Blessed are those who mourn, for they shall be comforted.

Why are these two statements back-to-back in Jesus' famous speech? Is it, maybe, because we who mourn are so, so poor in our spirits? That we need to be reminded that there is a *better* kingdom coming, a heavenly kingdom of which we are still a part even when we have literally nothing to bring to our King? Is it because in this poverty of spirit and season of mourning, we need the comfort of the only friend who can always see us?

In 2 Corinthians, Paul finally made the point in his crazy-talk that all the things he could boast about counted for nothing. That really his weakness was more worth boasting about because that's when Christ's strength could fill him.

I think I'm beginning to catch a glimpse of that.

I still don't have much to "bring" to God. Many days I am so sad, confused, angry, and just miss Elliot with a desperation I didn't know was possible. But I have a new awareness that bringing my "Nothing" to Jesus is enough. He doesn't ask me to be more or do more or have more. I've realized I can't generate any more. Only he can fill me with faith, hope, and love.

My little grain of sand is growing. It's not like it was, and it never will be again. I think maybe something purer will remain, free from the performance and religion I was so sure I didn't prop myself up with. I did. I can start to see that the wrecking of my heart and inner spiritual life, or the shattering of my mirror in an analogy I've used before, might leave room for a beautiful rebuilding.

At this point, though, I must reiterate something possibly controversial which I've alluded to in other articles. I think there is a misinterpretation that could arise while I talk this way about my faith being rebuilt into something new. I don't want to indicate that I believe God caused (or planned or willed) Elliot's death so that this could happen.

When Elliot first died, it felt just like God himself had come down from heaven to play a trick on me, that he cared nothing for me, that he cared nothing for Elliot, or perhaps that he didn't exist at all. These were lies. But then those lies gave way to other lies that said God wanted Elliot to die just to test me and make me more like Jesus. Like the price of my spiritual growth was my precious son's life.

What a bleak picture that paints of God. Thankfully, those lies are also beginning to be dispelled by truth.

I do not believe God allowed my son to die in order to make me more spiritual or refine me. If those effects do occur, it will show God's power despite this tragedy, not that God had to cause a tragedy to show his power. Just because God can make something beautiful from ashes, or fix a shattered mirror, or rebuild a demolished city, it doesn't mean he started the fire or smashed the glass or bombed the city.

I don't believe it was his will. He allowed it, and I don't know why, but that's a far cry from him "willing" it to happen. Believing that God mourns with me is necessary for me to move forward. It is another hope that lights up my grain of sand, and I can only believe He mourns with me when I release him from blame for causing Elliot's death. This isn't easy to do, but I'm working on it.

And this puts a little more perspective on Jesus' words in Matthew 5. Perhaps this is another reason Jesus is close to the poor in spirit, the mourners, the broken-hearted. His heart is also broken. Perhaps he cried out along with me the moment my baby boy died. When chatting with friends about this very topic, Jesus' response to Lazarus' death has come up several times. Jesus knew he was just about to raise his friend from the dead, and he still wept.

Commentators across the ages have speculated as to why this was, and surely there were many reasons. But there is a reason that is the clearest to me: Jesus Christ came to give life, and therefore he hates death.

Who knows how my grief journey and faith journey, which are very intertwined, will progress from here? I still have so many doubts and questions. "Normal" Christian routines like listening to WAY-FM in the car or church-going or even reading the Bible or praying still feel foreign. Sometimes I do those things and sometimes I don't, but when I do, I have no expectations. My impoverished spirit is very quiet before the Lord now because, like I said, I truly have nothing to bring. This isn't me being humble; it's just how it is.

Somehow in the depths of being so poor inside, I have found the glimmer of hope I was needing. Hope for comfort. Hope for the kingdom of heaven, and the day when death will never again invade our families or lives. Hope that light will dawn upon this dark night, and that, when it does, I will see Jesus more clearly than I ever did before.

Part Three: Mosaic

Chapter Eleven: Awakening

Desperation

As year two without my Elliot began, I continued ranting and raving in my personal journal, unfiltered and broken before a God I was not sure was even listening.

Last night, I told God we want to know him, not people's interpretations of him, not even one-liners from the Bible about him. Does he really show up for people? I don't want to be mocking or ungrateful for all we have but is there any way he can come and show us, tell us, reassure us: I am real. I do care. You are not alone. You will see your son again. Any way? God, I am crying out for this, and still, I am so, SO alone! —June 28, one year after

Driving home from Jill's, Sylvie says out of the blue,

"Mom, you'll never have another baby because your water broke, right?"

So innocent, so matter-of-fact. So piercing. I wonder if walking through the "pregnant lady" clothes at Ross made her think of that topic like it did me.

I will never have another baby.

"That's right," I said, "and that is a very big bummer," as my eyes filled with tears.

I will never have another baby. —July 14, thirteen months after

I dreamt of him last night. Kind of a recurring dream, I guess. Elliot's been in the hospital in the NICU this whole time, but he's alive. The doctors all say he's about to die, but he just keeps living. I'm with him. I can see him. I can touch him. And I keep feeling in awe that he just keeps living despite what the doctors say.

Maybe I dream that because that's kind of how I thought it would go.

The shock has worn off, and our son is still gone.

Since I can't have my son or my other babies, I beg God that I could have

him. Some comfort, some assurance, some hope that he's there and he loves me, and all will be well one day. I don't know what I'm looking for, but I feel like I'm spiraling further downward for not finding it.

Will I look back and see how he was comforting me? Am I missing it all because I'm just so damn angry and disappointed? I do have such amazing blessings…my children, my husband, my home, my family, and my friends.

But I also want Jesus. I think I want Jesus most. —July 16, thirteen months after

At this point, I was just getting so tired. Tired of hurting. Tired of being angry. Tired of pretending. Tired of missing my son. It felt like I was getting to a point of no return, where I would never find peace or happiness again. I was just sinking into despair, sleeping there, nesting in it. It had become a "carrion comfort," as Gerard Manley Hopkins calls it. It wasn't a healthy space to inhabit, but I didn't know how else to remain close to my Elliot. Trauma therapy for nine months had certainly helped my inner world, but I needed to do something that could be therapy for my outer life.

Finding God in Doing What God Does

Less than a year after Elliot died, my husband and I found ourselves in the process of becoming licensed foster parents. It didn't make much sense on the outside. Though I was desperate to have my little boy back, it wasn't some attempt to fill his spot.

It was hard for me to explain to others why we were fostering because I didn't entirely know. I wanted desperately to have some assurance that God was real and that Jesus cared. But I either felt completely numb when it came to God or still so very angry.

Why does my love for Elliot compel me to want to foster?

I've written about the fact that I would've endured those seven weeks of bedrest and so much more for Elliot. We would've lived in the NICU as long as he needed! We would've moved, sold our belongings, gone into crazy debt! I would've let them torture me to save his life when he was dying. Seriously, what would I have not done for my Elliot?

And are other children any less precious? Can I really say that I can't take one or two into my home because it might be hard? Or stressful? Or

inconvenient? Or because it might break my heart when they leave? Are those valid reasons to withhold my love?

I am trying to be open to my relationship with God, to hearing from him, to serving him. But I do not "feel" anything in regard to him. I don't think I'm going to find God in the Bible or church or reflection and feelings. I think I'm going to find God in doing what God does. —March 20, nine months after

I was achingly desperate for Elliot, of course, but also desperate for the presence of God. I had come to the point where nothing else would have been able to satisfy me. And God was about to show up in the person of a two-year-old boy.

I will never forget the moment the social worker dropped C off at our front door. He was the cutest little guy and not at all nervous about being in new surroundings. He bounced around like a pinball, getting into everything I wouldn't want a toddler messing with. We all just kind of observed him, unsure what on earth we'd been thinking. We weren't foster parent kind of people. But here we were, and here he was.

Before C came, I had worked out my little rituals of grief. I was comfortable reveling in my sorrow, likely too comfortable. C did not afford me any rituals whatsoever. He never stopped. I'd sit outside with him all morning while he buzzed around our backyard. I sat with him all afternoon while he repetitively fixated on a certain toy or activity. And I managed his outbursts and tantrums more frequently than I changed his diapers.

If I thought grieving and taking care of my two girls was exhausting, I had no clue what exhaustion meant until I was keeping up with our foster son. Keeping up with his meetings, his visitations, and his paperwork. Keeping up with him.

And now having a foster child is not just some hypothetical future event. C is really here, thank goodness napping, in the other room. It's been so hard, so crazy already, for all of us to adjust to. But he needs a good home, he needs structure and safety, and we will love him and do our best for him.

It's so strange to have him here and my Elliot not here! C came on Avery's second year due date. A two-year-old the day I was mourning my two-year-old I didn't get to bring home. I got the placement call for him while I was writing

in Elliot's journal. And he has Everett's middle name. It's like my babies were leading me to him, but it's so hard! I don't know this child; he's not really mine. I feel affectionate toward him sometimes, and at other times very irritated with him.

Today we went to that park I have such vivid memories of taking the girls to when I was pregnant with Elliot. Where I'd let them stand on my knee to look through the telescope because I didn't want to lift them too much. My Elliot has been to that very same park! And now it's C. This is so far outside my comfort zone. I don't feel like I'm naturally good with toddlers and preschoolers. And now, one is with me for probably months, calling me "mommy," looking for me wherever I go. I feel a little suffocated by him, and I think it's partially because I have not been used to this and partially because I get overwhelmed more easily since Elliot died. And yet, we're doing this! After the gift of deeper meaning and understanding Elliot gave us, how could we not do this?

I just miss him so. I hate that my loved, cherished little boy is in the ground, and the precious boy in the room next to me has not been loved and cherished the way he should have been. None of this is how it should be. Not for C, not for Elliot, not for me. I can't wait to go home and just be at peace. The peace is hard to find in these days.

One day at a time. I can only do this one day at a time. God, please be with me. Tell my baby boy how much mommy loves and misses him, and that I'll try to love him well by loving C well. —August 25, fifteen months after

The Defibrillator

The days passed, and I cannot say there was anything miraculous that occurred to suddenly awaken me from the deep sleep of grief and shattered faith. But I can say that having C was such a jolt to my system that I had to snap out of the comfort of the dark, at least some of the time, or I would have failed him badly.

In those crazy, mixed-up, busy months of fostering, I had little time to be sad, though grief still found ways to emerge. Sometimes when I'd drop C off for a visit with his mom and have a little time to myself, I'd let it all out, weeping yet again in my minivan. But then I needed to pull the grief inward, wrap it up, be present for C, and to still have plenty left to shower on Sylvia and Valerie. They all deserved the best of me.

I can say I loved C deeply, but sometimes he was difficult for me to like. For the first few months, and in the wake of some regressions, his behaviors could be very hard. And he took out the worst of those behaviors on me. He'd be sweet and compliant with everyone else ("He's such a sweet boy! He's just no trouble at all!") and then he'd scream at me and hit me and throw things at me.

There was an awakening in this experience. C lashed out at me, the person he called "mom," because I was the safest person he knew at that point in his life. All his anger, frustration, loss, and confusion that he could not possibly articulate was directed at someone who could show him unconditional love.

I remember a recurring incident where he'd ask for milk at naptime, so I'd give him a sippy cup of milk and he would hurl it across the room. "NO MILK!" So, I'd start taking the milk away and he'd scream, "MILK!" I'd give it back, and he'd throw it again. "NO MILK!" This happened many times. Many days. There was something raging inside him he had to get out. In my worst moments, I walked away in frustration. But in my better moments, I could see myself clearly in him, so I could see him clearly.

He was grieving.

And who better than I could understand lashing out all that grief disguised as anger on a loving parent?

I was C, throwing my milk cup at God over and over and over again. And God never chastised me. And God never disciplined me. And God never left me.

I would hold C after he calmed down (and after I calmed down).

I wonder, if I could look back and see with spiritual eyes, just how constantly I would see my Jesus holding me through every tear and every tantrum. How he was right beside me, right within me, in a more constant fellowship than I had understood.

Weeks turned into months with that little boy, and I did fall in love with him. He was a medicine I couldn't have known to ask for. My daughters became so used to him. Sylvia began our time with him referring to him as "our foster child," which became "my foster brother," which turned into "my brother." We could live and love again.

C's entrance into my life was not pleasant at first, and it shocked me like a bolt of electricity. But that shock woke me up, like a defibrillator, and my heart began beating again.

It's so like Jesus to use a child to do the best work.

Transforming

My journey of faith continued transforming as we fostered. Voices that spoke out in opposition to the status quo of evangelical culture's perception of God's will, God's plan, and God's sovereignty were becoming less of "crazy liberal Christians" and more like trusted friends. I didn't agree with everything they said, and I didn't have to. I agreed with the spirit in which they were saying it. My previous religious traditions had served me well for my first thirty-seven years of life. But now, those same traditions were cramming me in a box where I could no longer breathe. That religious box required God to talk to me in a certain way, to make his mysterious will known in abstract coincidences, to make sure that will came to pass, and to never, never be out of control.

The faith friends I found in my grief season did not put such demands on God. Though they offered many new ideas and interpretations, the theme I heard of their hearts was for the presence of God to be with them. I didn't realize it then, but that's also what my spirit was craving.

It was during our time fostering I made the unexpected discovery that I went to a Calvinist church. This was not in my new member packet. And I don't think it would have bothered me if it was. I try not to care much about the differences in theology we Christians carry around. But as this discovery collided with my ever-growing discontent with putting the blame of Elliot's death on God, it helped me pinpoint what was so off inside me in being at my church.

I did a little research into the associations my church was a part of, and sure enough, Calvinism was core to all of them. The people and leadership there are free to believe and teach any theology which seems right to them. But I was finally understanding it was just wrong to me. Calvinists somehow find beauty in the idea that God predestines who will choose Christ and thus have eternal life. I suppose they take comfort in believing that he wills all suffering to some greater plan or purpose. Perhaps before Elliot, I sort of believed all that by default. Now, well into my second year living without my beautiful son, my heart and mind expanding with a new and better picture of Jesus, these ideas were offensive to me and the memory of my son.

One sunny Sunday morning nearing the end of our time with this church, I sat in the pew and cringed when the topic of the sermon was announced: suffering. I had a feeling it wasn't going to be good for me. The sermon reached its climax around this Charles Spurgeon quote:

> It would be a very sharp and trying experience to me to think that I have an affliction which God never sent me, that the bitter cup was never filled by his hand, that my trials were never measured out by him, nor sent to me by his arrangement of their weight and quantity.[10]

The friend who was preaching went on to praise Spurgeon's perspective as a holy one, crediting God with all suffering and trials in each of our lives. I think his point was that we should be fortified in our trials by accepting they are blessings from God sent to try and refine us. And it's not a crazy thought, since the Bible makes statements like, "Count it all joy my brothers when you meet with trials of various kinds, for you know the testing of your faith produces perseverance" (James 1:2 ESV).

But the Bible also says things like this: "The thief comes only to steal and kill and destroy; I came that they may have life and have it abundantly" (John 10:10).

As with many doctrinal specifics, the Bible is not very specific.

My friend Ashley's baby boy Joshua died about a week after Elliot. Two separate mutual acquaintances put she and I in touch shortly after we buried our boys. I look back and see that her presence was given by God. I could talk to Ashley when I couldn't talk to God. I was so lonely so much of the time, but my friend Ashley was my one safe place, and I was hers. We cried together, we wrestled together, and we questioned together. We haven't always arrived at the same

10 Charles Spurgeon, "Metropolitan Tabernacle Pulpit," *Metropolitan Tabernacle Pulpit* (March 2, 1911).

conclusions, but that has never been the point in our friendship. The point has been that our boys, Elliot and Joshua, matter, and we matter. This friend was one of the tangible ways God showed up, though it took me a while to see it that way.

After that sermon on suffering, I wrote to her:

But I always wonder, does he really think that? That every 'bitter cup' is filled by 'God's hand?' Do the other church leaders think that? Like you and I have discussed, we have to all think of the implications of agreeing with statements like that! When we think of specific horrific suffering people go through, we cannot possibly think that! It's so easy to boil it down to a forty-minute sermon.

At one point, the preacher was listing 'suffering examples' saying things like, 'When your job isn't working out, when your relationships are struggling…' then inserted into the list, 'When a child dies…' Really? The death of a child makes a list like that?…It feels like it boils it all down to some trite, dumb life lesson. And Elliot is so much more than that. And God did not 'send me' the affliction of Elliot's death to show me some sort of love and tenderness. His love in tenderness, I believe, comes out of a heart of empathy that grieves WITH me over a loss He does not see as right, not as some test He sent me to refine me. I hate, hate, hate when people trivialize suffering like that." —September 18, fifteen months after

My mama's heart was compelled to protect Elliot's memory by not allowing blame for his death on God. I would not minimize Elliot's preciousness or God's love by falling into some misguided worship of "sovereignty." Though other bereaved parents may find comfort in believing God had their child's death planned, I found no comfort in that. And not only to protect Elliot's memory but to protect my own fragile beginnings of a trust in God again, I needed to push back against it. Whether or not this new perspective was "right," it was what I needed. And I needed distance from theology that kept ripping at my wounds.

The Calvinistic idea that God plans every event began to grate on me more while we had our foster son. Yes, God was using us in his life and using him in ours, but what kind of sick game would it be if it was all part of "God's plan?" For C's mom to be charged with neglect of her own child? For her to struggle to get her life on track so she could get him back? For C to be ripped from the only home he ever knew and placed in the home of strangers?

I would not believe that for C, nor would I believe it for me, or for Elliot.

I pictured my mirror analogy often as I'd grasp a sliver of light in the darkness. I envisioned myself sifting through the rubble of my broken faith, tossing most of it over my shoulder as religious nonsense. But then I'd find a shard, a piece of light that still shined, and I'd place it in a space above me. I began to think perhaps there would be pieces discovered in the ruins, and new pieces brought in, that could create something new and good, a funkier and more eclectic mishmash than my pristine mirror, but perhaps something more reflective of Christ. I slowly envisioned an outline of a mosaic where hope might live.

My pilgrimage commenced. Sifting through the rubble of my shattered mirror, I was on a hunt to find the slivers that reflected not religion, not church theology, not dogmatism, not my own understanding, but Jesus Christ and him alone.

Blog Post: "The 'God Is Good' Dilemma"

One and a half years after

God is good.

Chris Tomlin says it: "You're a good, good father…"

My childhood church camp said it: "God is soooo good, God is soooo good, God is soooo good, he's so gooood….toooo….me…." (four-part harmony)

The Bible says it:

"For the LORD is good; His steadfast love endures forever, and his faithfulness to all generations" (Psalm 100:5 ESV).

"The LORD is good, a stronghold in the day of trouble; he knows those who take refuge in him" (Nahum 1:7 ESV).

God is good.

But suffering is bad. Well, most people consider it bad. A few might think it is good because they think suffering is always sent by God as a test or a way to refine, so therefore the suffering is a good thing because it makes people how God wants them to be.

I don't think I think that.

Maybe in God's all-knowing realm, there are times when he directly deals out a dose of suffering because it is what someone desperately needs, like a loving family holding an intervention for an addict. But most of the time, I believe, suffering is exactly opposite of God's loving intention. We all know a lot of suffering is caused by our own foolish choices. But some of it is just no one's "fault." It just is, and it is not of God. I guess that's why Jesus' outreach was so much about alleviating suffering.

There is a dilemma when Christians want to hold on to the truth of the goodness of God, and accidentally get caught up in equating God's goodness with earthly blessings.

Here's what I mean. I have a good friend who also lost a son. Her son lived for two and a half months in the NICU. Then, finally, he was released to come home because the doctors believed he was stable enough to leave the hospital.

He died, in the middle of the night, next to my friend, in her room, a day and a half later.

Can you imagine that? Think of all the hope and love and worry that went in to seventy-nine days of drives to and from the NICU. Watching her son endure serious surgeries, observing helplessly as he was resuscitated multiple times before her very eyes, wondering what a life with his disabilities would look like, but not caring because of such deep love. Think of how relieved she and her family were to finally have their little boy at home with them. Think of my friend's other two children, proudly welcoming their baby brother home. Think of the joy and hope and anticipation and relief! Only for him to pass away in the night as they both slept. Let yourself imagine your child dying next to you.

That event is not good. Not even close! Not remotely! No matter what good ever comes from that sweet little boy's life and death, the fact of his death is a tragic loss than cannot be undone until eternity.

No Christian in their right mind would've said to her in the wake of her son's death, "God is good." That would've come across as insensitive and hyper-spiritual.

Now, seventeen months later, my friend is pregnant with another little boy. And you know what people have said to her when they've found out?

"God is so good!"

I get it. They're happy for her. They want to rejoice with her. They want to see beauty come from ashes because they probably know that she's been through a hell they don't even let themselves imagine.

And God *is* good. But is he good because of the blessing of a new baby?

She and I have talked about how the phrase can grate, and how we wrestle with the concept of God's goodness. When someone says, "God is good," in response to her being pregnant with another little boy, it is hard for her (and me) not to immediately think, "So was God not good when my son died?"

This is the dilemma.

God is good, yes. His blessings are good. But if he's good in the blessings, he's got to be good in the suffering.

While your new baby was born healthy, another woman in the hospital that same night might have had a baby stillborn.

While you and I slept warm and safe in our beds last night, hundreds of people within miles of us slept in the cold and don't know how they will eat today.

While I laugh and banter with my amazing husband, women around the world live in painful silence, afraid of the abuse their husbands heap on them.

While my precious daughters' most serious problems revolve around sharing toys, other little girls are right now held captive in sex trafficking, daily raped and exploited.

But God is...good?

He is. He must be, or nothing in the universe makes sense and existence is hopeless. But I don't understand his goodness. I don't understand how he can allow such evil and sadness and sorrow to exist. I don't like it. I get frustrated at him for it.

Considering this, I don't know why it's common to hear Christians say, "God is good," in response to blessings, in response to good feelings, in response to seemingly answered prayers. It's as if we've associated blessings with his goodness. To an extent, that's okay. I like my kind husband and precious daughters and cozy home. Thank you, God, for these good gifts. I do see God's goodness within his good gifts.

But God must still be good even if all these gifts were stripped away.

I don't get it. It's a dilemma for me to work out, and probably won't be fully worked out until I see him face to face.

In Lamentations 3, Jeremiah struggles with God's goodness. Do you ever wonder if we read the Bible confusedly because we can't see the passage of time it took an author to pen the words? We can't see the tears they might have shed as they scribbled on their scrolls. We can't see them rip up a parchment in anger or despair, only to start again once they returned to their Rock. Lamentations 3 comes across as ridiculously contradictory when read in one sitting. Honestly, I've thought if Jeremiah could really write that all down in thirty minutes, he was not super stable.

But what if it took him days, weeks, months, years to get to his turning point in verses 22-26?

I've been sitting with Jeremiah in the confusion and frustration of the first twenty verses of Lamentations 3 since my son died. Right now, I feel like I am beginning to dangle my feet off the ledge of verse 21. I'm not sure when I will be able to take the leap and land in the steadfast love of the Lord, but I know it's there. I know he's there. Ultimately, I believe he must be good…or else, what's the point of anything?

So, God is good. But even Jeremiah the prophet could not always see how that could be so.

"He has driven me and made me walk in darkness and not in light" (Lamentations 3:2).

"He has besieged and encompassed me with bitterness and hardship" (v. 5).

"…He has made my chains heavy. Even when I cry out and call for help, He shuts out my prayer" (vv. 7-8).

"He has turned aside my ways and torn me to pieces; He has made me desolate" (v. 11).

"My soul has been rejected from peace; I have forgotten happiness. So I say, 'My strength has perished, And so has my hope from the LORD'" (vv. 17-18).

Verse 21 (ESV):

"BUT…

this I call this to mind:"

Jeremiah, Jeremiah, Jeremiah. What can you possibly say? Where does your big "BUT" lead? You just said God put heavy chains on you and shuts out your prayer and has torn you to pieces? Seriously? What "BUT" can you muster?

Verses 22-25: (ESV)

> "The steadfast love of the Lord never ceases;
> his mercies never come to an end;
> they are new every morning;
> great is your faithfulness.
> 'The Lord is my portion,' says my soul,
> 'therefore I will hope in him.'
> The Lord is good to those who wait for him,
> to the soul who seeks him."

Dude, Jeremiah, I don't get it. But I guess that's what I want to get, what I'm seeking. It's this, the contradictory mess of Lamentations 3, that so well illustrates the dilemma I'm experiencing.

God is good. So many wonderful blessings in life are good. But there are spiritually dark seasons in which those of us who love God can't feel him or his goodness at all.

So, I do what I think Jeremiah had to do. He had to call to mind the goodness and love of God because the alternative is just too depressing, too hopeless. I think he really believed it, but in light of verses 1-20, it's clear he didn't always feel it.

God is good not because of all the beautiful blessings I have. God is good because in the end, all I have is him.

Chapter Twelve:
Fierce

"God is light, and in him there is no darkness at all" (1 John 1:5).

Another Goodbye

We were happy and sad we only got six months with our foster son. We were overjoyed that a family member came into C's life who was safe, appropriate, and loved C so very much. C lives with this family member still and is thriving. But we also grieved. We'd had another son. My girls briefly had a little brother. I had a little boy running around my house calling me "mom."

Near the end of C's time with us, he gifted me with a profound experience I'll never forget. I recorded that night in my journal:

C really got my heart tonight. I was playing games with him on my iPad, and anytime he looks at my devices (which all have Elliot as the wallpaper), he says, "There Elliot!" And tonight, I don't know exactly how it came up, but he wanted to see more pictures of Elliot. I have a folder in my photos on my iPad that is just an assortment of my Elliot pictures, so I opened that to show him. It was so precious yet so unusual how he sat there, cuddled with me on the bed, asking questions about every square inch of each of those pictures. I thought, I don't think any person except me has ever studied these pictures so closely. And of course, sitting there, looking at them in such detail, I started crying. Kind of abruptly, C got up and went into the living room and I thought, "Okay, he's done." But then, would you believe he had gone into the living room just to get me a Kleenex since I was crying? He crawled right up back next to me, handed me the Kleenex, and kept looking at pictures. He sat there for probably thirty minutes going through those pictures with me, asking questions and talking about every single one. This from the kid who can't sit still for five minutes of a TV show. It was very profound I think especially because it's so out of character for his rambunctious personality. It was weird. In a way, it was the closest I've felt to Elliot in a long time...maybe because I was cuddling with another little boy while I was remembering and missing him, maybe because I was reminded that loving C is loving Elliot, maybe because C's very perceptive tenderness felt almost like something spiritual...like Jesus and Elliot just wanted me to know I'm seen by them. I don't know. It really got me. —January 25, a year and a half after

The night we took C to live at his new home, my mama's heart was put to the test yet again. We had vaguely prepared him for this change, for the fact that when we dropped him off this time, he wouldn't come back to live with us. But he didn't really understand. Not until we were in that home, all his belongings in tote bags and a big box, and we began to leave did it dawn on him. Sweet tears and panic flooded him. He grabbed my legs, clutching my jeans. "I wanna go home! I wanna go home!" he cried. I couldn't explain to him, "*No honey. This is your real family. I was just your foster mom, and now that time is done.*" He wouldn't understand.

There are moments we can't understand what's happening. No explanation would ever be sufficient, especially against the backdrop of our fear and grief. I knew he was being placed in the care that was best for him.

But he wanted to come with me.

I returned to his empty room, sat staring at his bed, and I cried and cried and cried. Really, he stayed with us a short time in comparison to many foster care cases. But, like many events which change us forever, it carried the weight of a time much longer. I had been in such a dark place when C came to us, so dark it didn't seem light existed anymore. Somewhere in the absolute struggle of facilitating C into our lives and family, mitigating his trauma-laced outbursts, and allowing him to snuggle into the safety of my arms, my eyes began to sense light again. My heart began to feel something other than the rock-hard sorrow of Elliot's absence. It finally felt like I had the beginnings of a new me. While I wept, tears softened rather than hardened my heart.

Soul Care

A dear friend named Angela reached out to me soon after C left. She had recently begun living out a new calling as a spiritual director and asked if I'd be interested in meeting. Though C had helped thaw my heart toward God, my heartbeat still resisted him. I decided meeting with my friend couldn't hurt. At the very least, it was a good excuse to spend some time with her.

I began seeing Angela for soul care sessions once a month when Elliot had been gone for almost two years. At first, I felt nothing. I tried to complete the exercises Angela suggested, like reading a psalm and just sitting quietly with it, letting the Lord do whatever he would with it. Usually, my journaling went, "Yeah, I feel nothing for this."

My lack of feeling was not really an absence of emotion; it was a shored-up dam preventing emotions from flowing in or out. Any spiritual exercise that touched my emotions felt like trauma, like grief, like losing Elliot all over again. Though I no longer blamed God for Elliot's death and my misunderstanding of his promise, everything to do with God still equaled pain at that point. So, I bulwarked myself stoically against any feeling toward him. I didn't want to be tricked again into thinking I heard from him when all that danced in my head could just be the fabrications of my neural pathways.

Angela again reminded me that I wouldn't feel such a pushback against things of God if God wasn't there. My dammed-up energy was directed at someone, and he was allowing me to journey out of the darkness with no condemnation on me for all the time I spent there. In fact, he was with me there.

Does that seem incongruent with the way God is often portrayed? One of my least favorite preacher-y quotes, which I've heard many times over the years, is: "If God feels far away from you, *guess who moved?"* Oh really, preacher? In spiritual trauma, it is the victim of trauma who is to blame for a lack of feeling toward God? That if those encased in the dark night of the soul would just *try harder*, then God would feel close again? I think this is one of the most damaging messages that can be given to the spiritually traumatized.

It's true that God hadn't gone anywhere. But neither had I. I was the recipient of an evil, tragic event, and I did not (nor do you) have to be self-deprecating about my lack of feeling toward God (or negative feelings of anger, blame, and weariness). Physical trauma alters the body's ability to function; psychological trauma inhibits the rational abilities of the brain; spiritual trauma clouds the spiritual eyes with which we can see Jesus.

But just two years after such trauma, a weight of *it's your fault* still pinned me. I had emerged from many cages of religious convention, and still, the deepest, most subtle, yet iron-tight cage of misunderstanding holding me in was really this: God's love is *not* unconditional. We have to say the right things, pray the right things, believe the right theology, read the right Bible version, act the right way, abstain from sin, repent of sin, work hard evangelizing, and work hard serving. We have to *feel* a holy, praise-laced emotion every time we think of him. I see the topside of these messages as well-intentioned and truly devoted to the Lord. But in my own story, the underside was a bucketful of lies I needed to release. Maybe it's just me.

While I was meeting with Angela for soul care, I had dinner with a friend who loved me well through my dark night. She asked how I was really doing, and I couldn't get words out. Tears started spilling onto my Mexican food. She asked a simple question.

"Do you believe God loves you?"

I couldn't stop crying. She had asked it. She had said it out loud. And I, for the life of me, could not say yes. "I don't know," is all I could muster. I know she and others were praying for me to believe God's love for me somehow.

I think that you love me, God. Cathy asking me that at dinner last week hit a tender spot in me. But getting to talk it out with Angela a few days later was helpful. Because when I thought about it, I realized that your love is the only thing I know for sure….as the "world contends about its many creeds," it's almost humorous. People have been doing this for two thousand years and before! We don't know much. I'm clinging to the truth of your love. You love me. Maybe I need that. To sing "Jesus loves me" every day. It's okay if I use other things to cope. You still love me. It's okay if I have an off day. You still love me. It's okay if I "sin." You still love me. Until I have your love, none of it matters anyways.

Angela said she pictured me when she read the story of you feeding the five thousand. That your cousin John had just been murdered. And you were trying to be alone, but then a lot of "children" followed you. And you had compassion on them and met their needs, even though you were in the midst of your own grief. She said she saw me that way. I don't want to take that on because I know I'm a lot more selfish than that. But at the same time, I hope I can find that. I don't want to love my kids or my friends or neighbors or strangers out of duty or begrudgingly. The truth is, I know like I never knew before, that love is all there is. Maybe that's why sermons on duty or songs about how awful of a sinner I am just irritate me! I want the love of Christ to wrap me up, not all this religion.

"So if the Son sets you free, you are truly free." (John 8:36 NLT). —April 16, one year and ten months after

A Strange Conclusion

As I moved closer to acceptance of Christ's unconditional love, I became increasingly fierce in my protection of Elliot's memory and worth. Intermingled with this fierce protection was a determination not to paint God in the role of a cosmic torturer.

I'm trying to figure this out, but I haven't yet unraveled this mystery: why have we (humanity, Christians, religious, and nonreligious) assigned such dark attributes to God? When Jesus is "… the radiance of God's glory and the exact representation of his being, sustaining all things by his powerful word," (Hebrews 1:3a NIV), why do we not picture Jesus when we picture God?

The Bible is not clear-cut and easy to take as a cohesive whole, depending on what you expect from it. I understand there are many passages that depict God as separate, other, "holy," so set apart that our sinful selves could never be in his presence.

Enter Jesus, God-in-flesh, who was willing to put himself in the presence of sinners like us. So is Jesus, then, the nice side of God?

The conversations that could be started from this are many. Let me just say for myself that I have had to continually shift my view of God as less one that the ancients would have pictured: a far-off deity who loathes my shortcomings and must be appeased so I would not fall under his wrath. We Christians like to say, "God is love," but then we paint a picture to a watching world of a God who might as well be Zeus: a deity who commands utter obedience and eternally tortures pagans.

But our God does not look like Zeus. Our God looks like Jesus Christ, the exact representation of God, come down to us in the most utterly humble and accommodating way possible: as a baby who grew into a rambunctious kid who entered gawky adolescence and who emerged a man. This God, my Jesus, was not afraid to be in the presence of sinners like you and me. His love has always demolished barriers. His love has always reigned supreme. This God, Jesus, laid his hands on the sick and dying and healed them, calling those acts of healing to "destroy the works of the devil" (1 John 3:8 ESV).

This God, my Jesus, would not have willed the death of my little boy to serve some greater good. Jesus said that enemies come "to steal, and kill, and destroy," and yet somehow, our traditions have made God that very enemy (John 10:10 NIV). This doesn't mean I understand God's role in suffering, and I don't believe God is impotent. He does miracles, but maybe they are more subtle than we can always perceive. The shift from the darkness that engulfed me when I believe God let me down, that God lied to me, that God mocked my faith by letting Elliot die, to now believing Elliot's death was a great tragedy to his heart—this has changed everything. This is the shift that has allowed me to keep going.

I tell you, friends, I lived in the depths of doubt and darkness and soul-swallowing sorrow where all I had for God was vitriol.

And he loved me there.

And he loved me there.

And he loved me there.

Do you understand what I'm saying?

I'm saying if he loved me there, he loves everyone there. This changes everything.

Blog Post: "Not a Means to an End"

Two years after

My Elliot is not a means to an end.

A few months after Elliot died, a friend took me to lunch and asked me a provocative question. "Do you think it will ever be worth it?"

I wasn't offended. I knew what she meant. I would've wondered something similar prior to Elliot's death based on the way I viewed God then. The question came from a place of assuming that there must be something God is doing behind the scenes when a tragic event happens. Since "God is in control," there must be more than meets the eye when a child dies, when a loved one gets cancer, or when a maniac murders innocent people. And, along this line of understanding how God works, that means God must have a better purpose in his will for planning/allowing said horrors. I think what my friend was asking me was something like, "Will there ever be enough good to come out of Elliot's death that his death will have been worth it to you?"

I don't remember exactly what I said, but I know my answer could be summed up in one word:

No!

The moment Elliot died, I began a serious wrestling match with God, or what I thought was God. My raging screams of "Why?" permeated my ceiling, my car roof, and surely echoed into the streets of heaven itself. "Why?" seemed an appropriate question to a God in control. If he is in control of every minute detail of human existence, then on one end of the spectrum of control, he allowed Elliot's death (maybe the book of Job indicates Satan has to ask God's permission to terrorize lives?). On the other end of the spectrum, God specifically ordained/planned Elliot's death (maybe infant death was a good way to get King David's attention, and it was God's way of getting mine?). If he is in control, then what else could I ask him except, "Why?" Whether he ordained it or simply allowed it, he was culpable since it all must've been part of his "plan."

But somewhere along the way, after certain books and conversations and passages of Scripture challenged the assumptions that I was beginning with, I realized my wrestling match was not so much with God as with my theology. The theological starting place from which I began is, I think, where many Christians begin. My intention is not to cause controversy or debate, but rather to share my journey and perhaps elicit conversations.

Many mainstream Christians (I would venture a guess, though I may be wrong) probably begin with the simple starting point that

God is in control. Of everything. That was where I started. That's what was so comforting all throughout my life when things didn't go according to my plan, or when hopes and dreams were shattered. Well, I'd think, God is in control. If X, Y, or Z didn't go the way I wanted, God had a different plan, and his plan would prevail. The thought of God's control allowed me to rest night after night of bed rest in the hospital, Elliot growing in my belly, though his precious life teetered on the precipice of death at any moment. *God's got this*, I thought. *God has plans for Elliot, and nothing can thwart God's plan. God is in control.*

Even as I placed my hands on five-day-old Elliot as his life slipped away, praying through tears of frantic mother grief you cannot comprehend unless you have cried them, I clung stubbornly to God's control as the reason my boy couldn't die.

But he did die. Today, many mothers across the globe will watch life slip from their own precious children. The horror of it, friends—the absolute trauma and shock and helplessness of it—I've chronicled those things elsewhere. And if I still believed that all events occur with God's permission and according to his plan, I'd have to swallow the pill of believing God did that. God's master plan for my life included my precious son suffocating to death in my arms.

But I don't think that anymore. I don't think God's master plan for any of us is to experience the anguish of child loss or suffer from cancer or be trapped in addiction. It's never God's will for children to be abused by their parents and to be placed in the foster care system. It is not God's plan for drug trafficking to ruin life after life in my second home of Juárez, Mexico. It's not God's perfect will for children to be sexually exploited or for modern-day slavery to persist.

By Jesus, it is Satan who is called "the ruler of this world." By the author of Hebrews, Satan is said to hold "the power of death." A literal belief in Satan is not very popular these days, but, for me, when I think of the atrocities I listed above, no other explanation comes close. However, beyond the influence of Satan, we also live in what we Jesus-people call a "fallen world." It's not heaven, where God's will is always done. This is a place where other wills are often done—my will, your will, corrupted nature's will, unseen spiritual forces' wills. Why else would Jesus have taught us to pray for God's will to be done on earth as it is in heaven? Because he knew better than anyone that God's will is often not done here.

On the website ReKnew.org, author and pastor Greg Boyd defines this perspective more eloquently than I could:

> The warfare worldview is based on the conviction that our world is engaged in a cosmic war between a myriad of agents, both human and angelic, that have aligned themselves with either God or Satan. We believe this worldview best reflects the response to evil depicted throughout the Bible. For example, Jesus unequivocally opposed evils such as disease, demonization, and even natural disaster (i.e. Jesus rebuked the storm) as originating in the wills of Satan, fallen angels, and sinful people, rather than of God.
>
> This view is not ontologically dualistic, because while the Bible clearly articulates war between good and evil, it also clearly articulates God's sovereignty. The battle that is currently raging is not everlasting, and when it ends, we are assured of God's victory. In fact, the victory has already been won in the life, death, and resurrection of Christ (Colossians 2:13–14), but the demise of evil has not yet been fully realized. Christians are called to wage spiritual warfare (Ephesians 6:10–17) against evil through prayer, evangelism, and social action.[11]

I thank God for this revelation. Without it, I don't know where my wrestling match with God would have led me. Perhaps I would have walked away from my faith. Instead, I hold on to it that much more tightly.

Theology is a lot of educated guesswork, really. I don't think I have all the answers; I don't think you have all the answers. I don't think Martin Luther or Charles Spurgeon or C.S. Lewis had all the answers. I do think our striving to know God and understand truth are valuable endeavors and precious to our Father. We all just do the best we can with where we're at and what we can know.

My family and I are at the end of the monumental task of selling and moving out of our home of ten years. I wouldn't have undertaken

11 Gregory Boyd, "What is the Warfare Worldview?" *ReKnew* (blog), January 15, 2008.

this without a good reason, and our good reason (besides the fact that it is a *great* time to sell!) is so we will have adequate space to accommodate an adopted child. After we're situated in our next home, our plan is to begin the process of adopting from Colombia. Further down the road, we'd like to foster again. As we venture toward adoption, I wonder if I might hear comments like I did when we began fostering. Comments like these were hard for me to hear, well-intentioned as they were. I remember people indicating that our fostering was God's plan all along, using Elliot's death to bring us to that point. I respect my brothers and sisters who may believe that, even while I disagree. God's plan for Elliot was life. It is the enemy who comes to steal, kill, and destroy, not my Jesus. However, God would not let death have the final say over our family, so he did lead us to foster C and used our profound love for Elliot to spur us on. He did not allow Elliot to die so that we would foster C. And he did not let Elliot die so that we would pursue adoption. I believe God leads us to such things out of love that rebukes the evil of my child's death.

Elliot is not a means to an end. He was not an acceptable loss to God to accomplish something holier. He is my son. It breaks God's heart that a mother and her son are separated by death. And because God loves me, loves Elliot, loves each one of us so fiercely, he is constantly the warrior who fights to bring light out of the dark things of this world.

My wrestling continues as I struggle through things like the purpose of prayer and how to hear God. There's much confusion still jumbled in my mind, but there is also a certain measure of peace. I no longer cling to God's control as the solid ground on which to stand in the face of life's tragedies. I don't know to what extent God controls our world and our lives; I don't know if I'll ever know. But, in the end, I've found something more certain and tangible to cling to than his control.

I cling to his love.

Chapter Thirteen:
Unsurpassable Worth

Hitting "Reset"

Something reset when we moved out of our first house, an adorable little ranch we lived in for ten years. I didn't even know how many associations with grief and trauma I held there until we left. So much of it was good. The day we closed on the house, I stayed until the absolute last minute I had to leave to sign the papers. I actually hugged its walls, wept as I ran my hands around the doorframes of each room, and whispered, "Goodbye, old friend," as I exited the front door.

Goodbye old friend, where Dustin and I first learned married life, watched too many episodes of Star Trek and 24, and played Settlers of Catan with friends.

Goodbye old friend, where we brought home our first child, Sylvia, and stared at her in frozen wonder, so in love but terrified we'd break her. Goodbye old friend, where Valerie made her entrance into the world in a loud and bright fashion with a fire truck and ambulance. Goodbye old friend, home with a million memories of early parenthood: baby bouncers and bottles, blocks and highchairs, my girls' first steps and first words. Oh, goodbye, old friend.

Goodbye old friend, where friends and family had gathered, stayed overnight for visits, cooked out in our backyard. Goodbye old friend, where one precious family dog died, and a new puppy came to bounce around.

Goodbye old friend, where Avery Rose and Everett fell out of me silently in the little upstairs bathroom, without pain to my body but agonizing pain to my soul. Too silent and quiet for my world splitting in half. Goodbye old friend, the only house where I had them, ever so briefly, I had them. Blood and sorrow.

Goodbye, old friend, home Elliot should've come home to, home where Elliot existed inside me. Where I got the call from the Kaiser office informing me my blood test told Elliot was a boy. The house filled with him even after he was gone.

Goodbye old friend, where I sat on my office chair and realized my water had broken. House where I lay in the guest bed for two weeks trying to make it to the gestation when I could enter the hospital. House with that same bathroom where I bled on the floor, the toilet, and the bathtub with Elliot a dozen times, thinking I'd lost him again and again and again.

Goodbye old friend, where I built a scaffold of faith in the outcome, where dreams and words and hopes and fears mingled until I was certain I knew what God said and what the future would hold.

Goodbye, old friend, my house I returned to empty-armed and empty-wombed, staring at a crib that would never be slept in by my son.

Goodbye.

Remembrance

During our summer moving time, an infant loss organization who spoiled us well many times planted a tree in Elliot's memory. Extended family members joined us as we witnessed its planting. We'd been living in my parents' basement while we searched for a new house. We'd seen dozens and put in five offers without luck. Right after planting Elliot's tree, we visited a house that would become our new home. We put in the offer the same day, and the offer was accepted.

That day was exactly two years after Elliot's funeral.

Every act of remembrance, every "coincidental" date, every flower given, tree planted, and name of Elliot written, has imbued my mama's heart with good. Our family members gave us Christmas presents for Elliot the first year he was gone. Friends have given me so many gifts with Elliot's name. I've received jewelry with his name, hand-sewn blue birds and hearts with his name, birthday cards year after year for him. My dear friend Jessika's gifts of a windchime with his name and picture, and a children's book of his name, are permanent fixtures in our home. Sandra's photos were just the beginning of her many gifts of remembering Elliot and loving our family. Infant loss organizations have put his name on posters, t-shirts, and keepsakes. It hurts to hear his name and say his name, but it hurts more not to. Every time a loved one makes a gesture like this, it has been the arms of Christ. I am so grateful to the many friends and family members who've let God's love pour out through them in this way. Each overture of love rebukes death and shines life.

When a day filled with painful memories, like the anniversary of his funeral, can be reclaimed for something beautiful, I put Elliot in that beauty. He was only light and love and brilliance; a new reset allowed me to begin seeing the beauty of him beyond the pain of losing him.

Really Seeing

I read another couple of Greg Boyd's books that summer we moved into our new home. *Seeing is Believing* focused on the practice of imaginative prayer, a practice my soul care friend and others had encouraged me to try, which is also called "contemplative prayer." Boyd suggested using my imagination to talk with Jesus and made valid points that it wasn't hokey or New Age. Jesus gave me imagination for a reason. Boyd encouraged readers to picture themselves physically talking with Jesus in a setting that felt safe and familiar. Without too much deliberation, I knew where I would talk to Jesus. We were standing on my parents' gravel driveway on a moonless night, gazing at the stars together, as we did decades ago in my adolescence.

When I meet him in imaginative prayer, we are always there. Once upon a time, I would have found this practice very uncomfortable. At first, it felt silly and manufactured. Over time, however, I began to see that engaging my imagination was a beautiful way to "pray" that was much less manufactured than a list of holy-sounding praises and requests. I could see myself so much more personally loved and intimate with Jesus. He has done nothing but close the chasm which formed from religion, loss, and trauma. Now imaginative/contemplative prayer is just about the only thing that brings comfort. Usually, I simply sit in quiet and have these conversations with Jesus. Sometimes I write down the script of the prayer as it unfolds. And it is a beautiful thing.

And after I've been able to sit in and accept Christ's love for me, I feel renewed to accept Christ's love for every other person on this planet.

In another of his books I read that summer, *Repenting of Religion*, Boyd contrasts judgmentalism with love. It was another mind-blowing moment to think about judging in terms of anti-love. He says often how because Christ died for everyone, every single individual already has "unsurpassable worth." And if we look at our fellow humans in any way other than that, then we are judging rather than loving them. God warned against this in the garden in the metaphor of the tree of the knowledge of good and evil that separates you from me, good from bad, holy from profane, in from out.

I am more able to interact with all sorts of people than I did before Elliot. And not out of some secret plan to get them converted, to wait for the right moment to Jesus-juke them. But really, just because God sees me, I can see people better. I can see his love for me in my brokenness, and therefore I can see his love for them in their brokenness. I can see the absolute irreplaceable dignity of a little boy who lived only five days, so I can more easily see the dignity of a life, no matter its external appearance or behaviors.

Letting go of judgment (as much as I can; I am still very guilty of it) has helped draw me back to light. Seeing the unsurpassable worth of every human because Christ died for them removes a lot of pressure from placing expectations on others.

Along with being my irreplaceable little boy, Elliot is also a metaphor for all humanity to me now. As his mother, I esteem him with automatic worth beyond description. In my estimation, he is one of the most valuable human beings in all space or time, and I had the privilege of carrying, bearing, touching, and holding him. Was he valuable because of what he accomplished or contributed? Because of his righteous behavior? Because of his sound theology?

He was a tiny baby who never had the chance to grow into any of those roles. But he was and is a profoundly important person because he was and is my son. Because I love him.

And this—THIS! This is the love God the Father freely lavishes on all creation. Like Elliot is to me, we all are to God. Supremely cherished. Most valued. Irreplaceable. His children.

Oh, how bittersweetly I understand this now.

Never underestimate your worth. You are an Elliot to God. You cannot be replaced. You cannot be un-loved. You, *you*, are a child worth everything to your parent, not because of anything you do, say, or study, but simply because you are.

Blog Post: "A Boy Without His Mother"

Two years and four months after

My husband and I just returned from an unforgettable trip to Ireland in celebration of our tenth wedding anniversary. Trips like this are a memory overload, and soon after leaving the days of touring behind, all the landscapes and castles and fascinating history facts blend together. I'll take time to make a memory book on Shutterfly or something to separate and cement these precious memories. I'll lay my Shutterfly book on the coffee table, and it will likely not be interesting to many people except Dustin and me, and that's okay. It's the memories that are the real souvenirs, and these memories are ours.

The Irish people were kind and generous, and I think I enjoyed interacting with them as much as I enjoyed seeing famous vistas or landmarks. I've been trying to remain aware of the love of God in the present moment. In an extension of this, I've been trying to remain aware of the inherent beauty and worth of each individual I interact with and love them each in light of their worth within God's love. It was fun to really see people on this trip, really look them in the eye, really smile genuinely, and really listen.

Within the blur of memories that come with a week of jam-packed tours, talks, and tickets, there was one interaction I will have no trouble remembering. Dustin and I had just wrapped up our second day in Cork and were waiting at St. Patrick's Quay to board a bus to Dublin. We had about twenty-five minutes and set down our bags when Dustin mentioned he saw a young man on the sidewalk of the bridge who seemed to be crying. He confided he wished he knew how to approach the young man but didn't. I felt kind of lame that after all my insightful spiritual "seeing" people on this trip, I didn't notice this kid. Good thing my sweet man was doing the seeing for both of us. I asked my hubby to point him out. Sure enough, a young man, maybe eighteen or nineteen, sat fifty feet or so down the sidewalk. He had a black hoodie pulled around his curly mop of hair. His face was wet, red, and blotchy. He alternated looking out at the river, putting his hands over his face, and wiping his eyes. Now, lest I make myself out to be some sort of saint in this story, I must confess that my first comment back to my husband was, "Maybe he's high." Ah, judgment, how you like to jump the gun.

But we were concerned for the kid. I joked with my husband and said, "I'm going to do reconnaissance," as I walked down the sidewalk. I walked in one direction past the young man, turned, and observed. Yep. Real tears. I have cried enough tears in public places to know that not much besides grief or trauma could cause anguish like that. My heart was immediately with him.

I approached him and bent down. "Are you okay, honey?"

He shook his head. Man, just writing this, I'm thinking how brave he was! He could've austerely wiped his eyes and pretended. He could've acted tough to the American tourist twice his age. But, wow, he had the courage to open up to me!

"I missed my bus."

"You missed your bus?"

Okay. My mind went into problem-solving mode. Does he need money? Help? What?

"Yeah," he said, "And my parent died."

A familiar heaviness grabbed my heart. "Your parents died?"

"No, no. One parent. My mom. My mom died. I just found out. And I missed my bus, so now I have to wait for the 5:00."

You know, this intermingling of sorrow and joy we all endure on our journey to eternity is so profound that I almost don't have words for it. Really. I'm having a hard time continuing as I recall this moment. I had just enjoyed a fun, goofy rainy day with my husband, kissing the Blarney Stone and riding a double-decker bus. And at the same time, this young man had lost his mother and was stuck after missing his bus back home.

I've thought before how surreal it is that the moment my son Elliot died in my arms, people were out having dinner or watching TV or driving or laughing. How could people do those things while my little boy was dying? Of course, I know that's a futile line of thinking, but those of you who've experienced a life-altering loss or trauma probably know what I mean. It's hard to accept that an event that changes our universe forever did not, in fact, change the universe.

I sat down by this brokenhearted young man. "Oh honey, I'm so sorry."

I asked permission to hug him. He nodded. So, I put one arm around him and used my other hand to rub his back. It was intimate, but it was okay. I asked, "What happened?"

I learned my young friend was named Jordan. His mom had had cancer and had been in the hospital. He lived in a different city, going to school.

"I was meant to go up there earlier today, but I stayed to finish some school stuff." His teeth clenched, and heaves began wracking his body as he cried out to me, "I should've been there!" He'd last seen her a week prior.

Oh, sweet Jordan. The agonizing regret I know so well. If I had been there, done more, stayed, paid better attention, *should have, should have, should have.* I know. I told Jordan I'd lost a son and that I understood the shock and incomprehensible pain and all those self-blaming thoughts. I understood, and I also knew there was nothing I could say to make him feel better.

I asked a few more questions and listened as he spoke. His mom's name was Brenda. She was a chef. When I asked about his dad, Jordan simply said, "He left." I asked if there were siblings or other family somewhere. He told me he thinks he has some brothers somewhere, but he doesn't know them. It was just him and his mom. Like most of us, I didn't know what else to say. This boy had lost the one family member he had in life! What else was there to say?

So mostly, I just sat with him, letting him cry, crying with him, rubbing his back, and saying, "I'm so sorry, honey."

I cried for his loss and the crappy way it happened. I cried because it was a trigger sitting with him and opening my heart to the pain of another human being's trauma and loss. Everything beautiful in Ireland had made me ache more than I can say for my Elliot because all things beautiful remind me of him. It hurt to sit there with Jordan! And yet it was perhaps one of the holiest experiences of my life.

After sitting with him for ten minutes or so, one arm around him, the other hand rubbing his shoulder and back, I tried to gauge if I was making him uncomfortable. I wondered if maybe he was thinking,

"Okay, lady, thanks, but this is getting weird."

But as soon as I wondered, Jordan suddenly angled toward me and put both his arms around me. Friends, he grabbed on tight in the familiar way you would with your own mom or dad or sibling or best friend when you needed a serious hug. He clutched my clothes and wept into my shoulder, all his precious snot and tears pouring onto my sweatshirt. I loved that boy very much at that moment. In any other context, I'd bet Jordan is like any ordinary young adult, and he and I would barely notice each other on a sidewalk, separated as we are by age and gender and nationality. At that moment, though, I felt I was just holding a boy who missed his mother and who just needed a mom to hug. I think I also needed a son to comfort. A boy without his mother and a mother without her son, embracing there on the River Lee. Thank you, Jordan, for entrusting me with such a sacred space. I felt Elliot there.

Jordan released his tight hug, and I sat with him for a few more minutes until my bus started to board. I got his number in hopes of checking in on him. I told him I'd pray for him and encouraged him to grab onto someone in his life to share this burden of loss with. It didn't feel like nearly enough.

What will the coming days and weeks and months hold for Jordan? I wish I knew. I haven't received responses to the texts I've sent him, so maybe I'm doing international text wrong, or the number is off, or maybe he would rather forget our interaction. In any case, he's here in my heart and prayers. Maybe you'll say a prayer for him too.

I had so much fun on this trip to Ireland, and I also cried much. Sorrow hovers at the fringes of joy in my heart. Feeling one almost always leads to feeling the other. I'm trying not to overthink that but accept how it is for me is often how it was for Jesus: sorrow and love flow mingled down.

Jesus has shown me lately that I, like Jordan, am quite loved by Christ in my grief. I am loved when I'm laughing, making memories with the man I married. I am loved when I am in a hole of trauma that makes me unable to see anything but the hurt. I am loved when I believe and so loved when I doubt. Jordan's tears that day were very beautiful to Jesus. Blessed are you who mourn.

I'm glad I met you, Jordan. I'm so sorry for this sorrow in your life. You should not have lost your mom way before her time. Thank you for the beautiful honor of comforting you. In this way, Jesus reclaims the wrongness of the deaths of our loved ones and uses our broken hearts to do something lovely. I'm thankful for a few minutes I was able to hold you, another mama's little boy, since I cannot hold my own little boy anymore.

And of all the beauty there was to experience in my holiday away, you, Jordan, were the most beautiful thing.

Chapter Fourteen:
Live and Move

Like Fireflies

"Darkness, stop bullying me!" I shouted at the gates of the cemetery. "*Light wins!*"

I have shouted and screamed and cried so often upon entry to that cemetery, I'm probably known as crazy-screamy-minivan-mom to the groundskeepers.

But that day, I was in a fight with the dark. I was so sick of feeling like I had no control to actually enjoy my son, to remember him with energy and hope, rather than draining despair.

So that spring day nearing three years after Elliot's death, my soul care session had fueled me to not give up without a fight.

It was the day before COVID-19 shutdowns in our state, right before the world got even weirder than usual.

I began my time with Angela that day, and I knew it was a day I needed to talk about Elliot. I knew I had to talk about him because just thinking about him brought the searing pain of tears to my eyes and a balloon of grief into my chest.

"I don't know how to keep moving without feeling like I'm leaving him behind," I told her. "I don't know how to remember him without feeling so, so heavy."

She's great at listening. She doesn't spout cliché phrases or trite solutions to suffering. She just invites God in. She asked if she could pray, and when she did, she said, "God, we know you are with everyone in the world, in all their suffering and struggles, but you are with us just as much in this room."

Bible verses don't come to me as frequently anymore, but while she prayed, the words "for in him we live and move and have our being" flashed through my mind (Acts 17:28 NIV). Even now, after the fact, I can't explain it, but I can only say it was a moment of "getting it." Of truly comprehending that Jesus was with me in that room. I pictured a million pinpricks of light all around me as his presence, light that is always there but which the darkness of this world has made so hard to see. I felt like I was swimming in a florescent pool, and at that moment, I wondered how I could ever not see the light of Jesus. And I couldn't help but be in that NICU room again, seeing me there, holding my beloved baby boy while he died. And the pinpricks of light were there, too. There in the darkest dark. Jesus was even there.

As Angela and I began talking, I shared with her what I had pictured while she prayed. "Like fireflies," she said. I liked that. Like fireflies.

"I'm so sick of the darkness always shrouding Elliot. I feel a strange hope and determination to reclaim his memory in the light."

Angela nodded as I explained what a relief it would be if Jesus could bring light back to my memories of my beloved son. Think of your children running around your home right now. Wouldn't it be a tragedy if every time you thought of them, you were also triggered to the worst moment of your life?

I was planning to visit Elliot at the cemetery after my session with her. "When you visit the cemetery, is it light or dark?" she asked.

I almost scoffed. "Dark," I said without a beat. Then I paused and finally said, "But even that place, I want to reclaim in hope and light."

She handed me colored pencils and asked me to draw things in my life that I felt were in the light and which things were still in darkness. So, I drew a Bible in the light and a tree representing nature because I feel like I have openness toward those things again. I drew a building that was a mix of the building we had Elliot's funeral and a church in the dark. And wrote Elliot in the middle. I then thought I was done, but I realized I wanted to add something that showed I do believe God is somehow there amid it all, the dark and the light, no matter how I feel. So, I drew a sun encapsulating it all, the dark and the light, even though I didn't feel Christ yet in the dark places.

Then when I was done, before she looked at my picture, she read me this passage:

Where can I go from Your Spirit?
Or where can I flee from Your presence?
If I ascend to heaven, You are there;
If I make my bed in Sheol, behold, You are there.

. . .

If I say, "Surely the darkness will overwhelm me,
And the light around me will be night,"
Even the darkness is not dark to You,
And the night is as bright as the day.
Darkness and light are alike to You.
(Psalm 139:7-8, 11-12)

I looked at the picture I'd just drawn and saw how I had put God's light and presence symbolically in both the light and the dark. Darkness and light are alike to you. It was like he had just told me what she was about to read to me from Psalms. I haven't had many moments since Elliot died of feeling like God was doing something so clear that he didn't want me to miss it, but that felt like something.

And the truth is, yes, I always, *always* doubt whether an experience like this is really God. After the trauma to my spirit that occurred when I believed God promised my son's life, how could I not doubt? The difference which slowly crept up on me over these years of wrestling is that my doubts used to be bitter cynicism. They gradually morphed into annoyed itches I'd scratch away. As Christ continued to meet me in darkness with his love, void of judgment or religion, he softened my own response to doubt. I suppose a little like Paul states in 1 Corinthians 4: "I do not even judge myself" (v. 3, NIV). Now, my doubts are just part of my faith, and I sit in them the same as I sit in my convictions and certainties. After all, is faith that must be certain truly faith at all?

As we concluded our soul-care session that day, Angela asked me what we could do to prepare me to go to the cemetery. I told her I wanted to tell darkness to stop stealing my memories of Elliot and making them dark. I even wrote it down: Darkness, stop bullying me. LIGHT WINS.

I took that with me as I drove to visit Elliot. I envisioned that light, like fireflies, all around me. I turned on an album by a band called Mae, which usually brings my spirits up. As I turned the corner into the cemetery, this line from the song "A Race for Our Autonomy"[12] came bursting into its final crescendo:

I see you catching onto me
And with it you should know
There is a hope where none should be
And time for letting go
It's giving into honesty
And taking back control
A race for our autonomy
A heart that's full of hope

And I swear I could see Jesus' light like fireflies surrounding and bursting through the roof of the chapel near the cemetery's entrance where Elliot's funeral was held. I smiled thinking of Elliot, who is with Jesus in that light, and with me all the time, choosing to believe I was going to his special place out of celebration for him that day, not out of despair. Despair has come again, but that day there was victory against it.

Elliot and I took a nice walk that day. His light inspires me to be better than I sometimes want to be. It is still so hard missing him. But that spring day before COVID-19 upended normalcy, I received a very meaningful reassurance that no darkness can stamp out light. It's just that the light is so hard to see sometimes.

A New View of the Same Stars

In the evenings, I often step out on the patio of my home to find my bearings. The North Star. The Big Dipper. Follow the arc to Arcturus and speed on to Spica.

There, my friendly star still greets me and reminds me of a younger me, full of wonder and anticipation about what life would bring. I'm still staring at Spica and hovering with that blue star. I recently researched Spica and discovered it is, in fact, a binary star.

12 Mae. "A Race for Our Autonomy." *3.0*. Tooth & Nail Records, 2018.

Two stars dancing wildly in space in the unalterable ties of gravity. Wikipedia states, "Spica is a close binary star whose components orbit each other every four days. They stay close together enough that they cannot be resolved as two stars through a telescope."[13]

Close enough together that they are only seen as one entity. Maybe this is what Jesus has been teaching me. I am not void of his presence, not ever, not in the most hellish nightmare of my life. Not when I am raging against God or cynical or bitter. The gravity of his love keeps me encircled to him so much so that we are never really a separate entity. That means what I feel, he feels. The tragedies and traumas I suffer, he suffers with me. The joys I celebrate, he celebrates with me. I couldn't see it for a time. For a time, I felt it was the opposite—that he was as far from me as our little pale blue earth is from the stars.

But I am in him, and he is in me. This is how I know he loves Elliot even more than I can. He is the best of me, the most loving of me—how could he do anything less than fiercely also love my son?

On Elliot's third birthday, a friend sent me a flowering plant in remembrance of him while we were away on our "Elliot trip" to celebrate our boy. My neighbor held on to the plant until I returned. I was so moved to see a little blue bird nestled in the leaves and flowers. Most people who know our story know a bluebird is the symbol we use for Elliot. It began with a picture frame I bought to display a photo of him at his funeral. I began thinking of him as my "little bird." Simultaneously, my dad wrote a poem for Elliot just days after he died with two bluebirds printed on the paper, and began with the words, "Where are you little Elliot, and why did you fly away?" After that, my song, "My Little Bird," formed in my head. I wrote a children's story in honor of Elliot and my friend Ashley's son, Joshua, in which Elliot Bird and Joshua Fish forge an unlikely friendship. And when a bluebird flies by or lands in my view, my whole body is flooded with joy and missing my son.

So, when my friend Leslie sent a plant with a bluebird, it was the sort of kind and intentional thing she would do. I texted her to say thank you and said I especially loved the bluebird.

"I didn't order any bluebird," she said. There wasn't even an

13 "Spica," Wikipedia (Wikimedia Foundation, September 2, 2022), https://en.wikipedia.org/wiki/Spica.

option for her to include something ornamental with the plant.

I stared at that little bird in the plant from my friend and just wept. Yes, it could have been a coincidence. And as I've said, my first inclination is to doubt anything is a "God thing." But I am working toward no longer allowing my cynicism and pain to wash away hope. That bluebird is a little sliver of light sent to me from Elliot and Jesus. I can't prove it. I can't explain it. But I will have it. I will take it as light. I will take it as hope.

This is what it means to have walked this road. It is not some fluffy one-liner that can soothe trauma and soul-searing loss. It is years of the pit of hell, and God never, never, never once giving up on me or telling me I was too much. This is why I can still come to him. This *un*conditional love is what I am in for. I don't understand why Elliot died. I never will. It will never be okay, there will not be enough good to come from it that will make it worth it.

But a little bluebird on his birthday reminds me: this cannot be all there is. There is more. There is more. There is more.

In an imaginative prayer session soon after receiving that little bluebird, I wrote out my conversation with Jesus like a script—something I don't normally do, but what I pictured in my conversation with him was so vivid that day that I just had to write it down.

Journaling Imaginative Prayer

Three years after

Me: This life goes really fast, doesn't it?

Jesus: (nods) Cherish it, but don't hold on to it.

Me: All I can do with this time is love well.

Jesus: And be loved well by me.

Me: I want my adoptive baby.

Jesus: I know.

Me: I miss Elliot so much it hurts.

Jesus: I know.

Me: What do I do with it all?

Jesus: Know you are loved. And love.

Me: I will try. Some days are so hard. Some days are so heavy.

Jesus: I'm with you on every kind of day. You also need to love yourself, especially on the hard days.

Me: Thank you for showing me a different way about you.

Jesus: I'm sorry it was such pain that taught you. It is for many.

Me: You didn't do that, did you?

Jesus: No. That's not what I do or who I am.

Me: You never left us, did you? Me and Dustin? Elliot?

Jesus: Never.

Me: I wish I could see Elliot.

Jesus: I know. When you look out there, you see him. I am in everything, and he is in me. He is closer than you think.

Me: And Avery and Everett?

Jesus: Yes.

Me: My adoptive child somewhere in Colombia right now?

Jesus: I see them all. I am with them all.

Me: Just don't leave me.

Jesus: Never.

Blog Post: "Of Plans and Pandemics"

Three years and three months after

I sit here admiring the frosted trees, the still beauty whispering something majestic and true. A September snow blew through to hopefully temper wildfires and delight Coloradans with the dramatic weather shift. It's funny how we live our lives with an awareness that things rarely go as planned, and yet we're still surprised when an out-of-season snowstorm rolls in.

I remember about five years ago daydreaming with my husband about adding a third child to our family. That's all we knew: we could daydream it, plan it, and it would happen. It's sweet and sad to me now how simple that seemed to be. I knew life did not promise to unfold so seamlessly. But dreaming is what people do. We can't sit around expecting disappointment or dreams would never be pursued.

So, we pursued the dream of adding a biological child to our family. And, as you know if you know me at all, the dream was dashed twice with miscarriage. I think of those babies, Avery and Everett, buried in tiny caskets on my parents' property. They were all the potential of life, of a little sister or brother for Sylvia and Valerie, of another lively voice filling this house. They weren't dreams, and they weren't mistakes. They were my children. They *are* my children. Avery would be four years old now. What a wonder that would be, a precious little her. I wish I knew her.

The dream swelled bigger than ever before during my pregnancy with Elliot. After the agony of burying two babies, no words express the ache inside me to keep Elliot safe. My body betrayed me, however, and tried to miscarry him nearly every week. Every miracle that kept him alive through the nightmare of that pregnancy gave me a fiercer determination. He would come home. He would live. Sylvia and Valerie would not endure the loss of another potential sibling. Dustin and I would not endure the loss of another child. Our little boy would grow up! Through nearly two months of lying in a hospital on bed rest, trying to ensure his best chance at life, hours of listening to the music of his heartbeat on the monitor, with nothing but his kicks in my belly to keep me company, I believed the dream would absolutely come true.

And if you know anything about me at all, you know that did not happen. My precious son was born, lived, and died unexpectedly when he was five days old. Did you know still, over three years after he died, I often wake up with aching arms? Did you know that's what it's like to lose a child? To feel the heavy disbelief of him not being here assaulting me anywhere, anytime? Child loss is not an acute pain that passes. It is chronic, ongoing, with good days and bad days. It is a new normal.

So, it was within this new, painful normal that we somehow found the strength to dream again. We became foster parents, not really knowing where that adventure would lead. Our precious, priceless experience of briefly fostering confirmed two things. One, that even after the unimaginable loss and trauma of losing Elliot we still had room in our hearts to love another child, and that child did not need to be born from my body. Two, we were not ready as a family to foster long-term and endure more loss upon loss. Our little girls had endured too much trauma and loss already. The death of their little brother Elliot has become interwoven into their life stories, and I will do what I can to protect their precious hearts from enduring too much too soon.

International adoption had been a dream in my heart since young adulthood, though back then, I had some naïve perceptions of it. After saying goodbye to our foster son, everything pointed toward international adoption as our next step. So, we made big changes. We sold our house and bought a bigger one. We researched and prayed and decided on Colombia as the country. We picked an adoption agency. We applied and paid them boatloads of money. We got started about a year ago, wondering and dreaming about who the child would be and when he or she would come home to us. I remember wondering, hoping, "Will it be maybe by next summer?"

And a heavy whisper of my new normal cautioned me away from too much optimism. Life does not promise to go smoothly. Dreams sometimes are realized, sometimes they are delayed, and sometimes completely dashed.

My grief journey has been a wrestling match entwined with a journey to rediscover God in a new light. It's been beautiful sometimes and painful and ugly other times. It's a journey that is far from over. Most of what I thought I knew has been decimated, but I know one thing much more clearly. I know God is love. I picture the confusion and unanswered questions regarding a million aspects of God, the Bible, and Christianity swirling around me like a swarm of angry bees. But in the center of that chaos, I sit quietly, untouched and unhurried, safely encapsulated in his love. It is all I know for sure and all I need to know ever, really. And when something about reality seems incongruent with God's love, then I do not try to reconcile it. I do not try to explain it away with a religious cliché. All I do is try to become more still in the love and presence of Christ, usually in the practice of contemplative prayer. It's all I can do.

And that is all I can do with this…this…what do we call a global pandemic? A nightmare, maybe? Not that beauty has not emerged from COVID; it has. In my job as a home study writer, I get to interview the most interesting people and hear their life stories, past and present. A theme I've been hearing lately is how, alongside the difficulties and tragedies COVID has produced, many people have found a quiet place. They've had more time at home, more time with family, and more time to focus on the blessings right in front of them. They've grown closer to their spouses and children, sometimes through plenty of conflict and irritable days. Maybe like 9/11 did decades ago, COVID has shaken us from our stupor and awakened us to see what a precious gift each healthy, happy day of life is.

But where I want to count blessings, I also want to acknowledge pain. I don't think it's right to elevate one at the expense of the other. COVID has caused pain in so many aspects for so many people; I couldn't list them all. I believe God, in his love for us, can be with us through the pain and eventually bring something beautiful into any human story. Yet I also believe he weeps with us for what we lose in this life. Whether we lose a loved one, a dream, time we should've had together, or hope, Christ sits alongside the suffering.

In November 2019, our adoption agency posted the picture of a little boy, "Baby Joe". There is just no overstating his cuteness. The same day, a dear friend also saw his picture on a different forum and immediately shared it with me. When I researched his needs, I was overwhelmed but not deterred. I requested his file. I'll never forget reading it in my bedroom that night, overcome with emotion. I cried so much for that little boy, for his birth mom, and for the fact that I knew we were so early in the process that I wouldn't be able to get to him for months. I didn't even know if my husband would be on board with pursuing him or if a different family might put in a letter of intent for him first. I didn't know. All I knew was that I felt intimately connected to his story, and that night ten months ago, I would've gladly hopped on a plane to get him.

And the months passed. Each month, I'd daydream about when the next step would finish and what that would mean for the step after and the step after. But each step took so much longer than I'd hoped. I remember daydreaming around Christmas about how amazing it would be to get to Colombia to get Joe before he turned two in March. But our home study wasn't even completed and submitted until mid-March. *Finally, finally,* I thought! This is really where things can start moving! *After we submit our home study, we just have to jump through a few more hoops before we can submit our dossier, receive a referral, and get a date scheduled to travel!* I even let myself imagine it could still happen in the summer.

A week after we submitted our home study for review and approval by the U.S. government, of course, you know what happened because it happened to you, too. Your kids were suddenly remote learning while you were trying to work from home. You tried not to freak out about the lack of toilet paper, but you couldn't help but snatch up a spare roll when you saw it. You longingly looked at playgrounds with caution tape surrounding the equipment and wished your kids could play. Maybe you were furloughed or laid off. I know it didn't affect just me. But at the same time that those things were happening to you and your family, internationally adopting families felt their worlds come to a screeching halt. Some families got trapped in foreign countries. Some were days or even hours away from flying to pick up their children, then flights stopped. Some people, like us, were in process of a step that shut down because all the relevant government offices shut down.

All that hope that was building in me for the next step of the adoption process seemed to melt through my fingers, and a familiar disappointment took its place. The submitting of our home study to the U.S. government, some fancy fingerprints that went along with that, and an approval letter—this process should have taken six to eight weeks. And now, thanks to COVID-19, this process is going on six months. I check my mailbox obsessively for the final authentication of that approval letter to come in the mail so I can send it to my agency and finally submit our dossier to Colombia. This should have happened months ago.

This is life in a world with such a mix of beauty of pain, light and dark, hope and disappointment. You hope to have a baby, and you experience infertility or miscarriage or the death of a child. You hope to have a career you love but feel trapped in a job you hate. You hope for a lifetime of happy married years but struggle each day even to like your spouse. You excitedly and nervously hope for a timeline to bring a child into your family from across the world, then the world abruptly changes. These disappointments are real, and these disappointments are hard.

And still, in this uncertainty, there are such displays of Christ's love and light, I know he cannot be far off. Around the time of Elliot's birthday and the anniversary of his death in May and June, I kept thinking of "Baby Joe," whom we now refer to as Little J, every time I wept for Elliot. In my moments of quiet contemplation with Jesus, when my mama's heart was breaking again for my Elliot-bird, for my son whose birthday we'd celebrate but who wouldn't be with us, I kept seeing Little J's face. It felt as if Elliot was there in those quiet moments, bringing Little J's face to mind, gently encouraging me to be brave. To lay out my mama's heart again in hope for the future and move forward.

My husband, who'd been hesitant about Little J's medical needs, felt something shift in him around the same time. Dustin said one night after we watched TV, "I think we should put in a letter for him." So, in mid-June, seven months after we'd first seen Little J's file, we submitted a letter of intent to Colombia. Our agency caseworker said it could take a week or two to hear if they'd approved it. But the very next day, she called to tell me it was already approved. This did nothing to speed up all the shutdowns and the suspended animation of our adoption process, but it meant we were now the family reserved for Little J.

Just a few days after we knew our letter of intent was approved, we held a fundraiser garage sale for our adoption. It still humbles my heart to remember the friends near and far who came by to love and support us and pay way too much for lemonade and baked goods. Strangers, too, when they heard we were raising money for adoption, refused to take change for their items. That weekend was like a hug from heaven, all of you wonderful people who supported us and keep supporting us, reminding me that God does not cause disappointment and disease and dashed dreams. But he is always, always, always with us during those difficulties.

It's been nearly three months since we put in our letter of intent for Little J. We have inched along in the process as offices have slowly opened, backlogged though they are. COVID has affected our adoption timeline, and I think this is sad. I've had people tell me God is teaching me patience through this, and all is happening in God's timing. Though I trust God will be with us and our child, and I believe he can do beautiful things with this, I reject the assertion that this is his "timing." God doesn't cause worldwide pandemics and keep children from their forever families for months or years longer than necessary. Little J could have already been here, getting to know us and us getting to know him. How I wish he was.

All this waiting is challenging, but I fully expect the challenges to come will dwarf what I'm experiencing now. And that's why I want to get started. I struggle every day to have patience with my daughters, to homeschool them without wanting to hide in a closet for half the day, and to keep my cool when they give me one of "those" looks. And of course, snuggles, giggles, and genuine joy punctuate even the hardest days. This is real relationship.

Every day that passes without Little J is a painful trigger of what it's like to live without Elliot. Elliot is perfect, but he shouldn't be. He should be a whiny three-year-old who fights with his sisters and gets hangry. He should need me constantly and wear me out. But instead, he's a cherished memory and a set of pictures around my house. So, when I see our year-old pictures of Little J, and that's all I have, it's like I have two sons who are just two-dimensional pieces of paper. Another little boy whom I want to wrap my arms around but can't. A little boy who is "perfect" in my mind but shouldn't be. I want him here with all the challenges another child in our family will bring. I want the mess, the mix of laughter and lullabies, tantrums and tattletales.

So, I guess I keep dreaming. I keep planning. I keep hoping. But there is a caution in this hope. It almost didn't surprise me that something ridiculous like a pandemic happened the year we decided to adopt internationally. We all live in this tension daily, a dichotomy between perfect and pain, and even the weather doesn't submit to our plans. We're not living yet in the realm where dreams never die. So, if more dreams die, if more heartache comes, and when more joy fills this house, whatever comes, it will be God's love I find myself in.

This doesn't mean life will be perfect or go as planned; it simply means I will never be alone.

Chapter Fifteen: Estrella

Bogotá, Colombia

Four Years After

The bustling noises of Bogotá overwhelm my senses as I push my newly adopted son in his stroller to the relative calm of our hotel courtyard. We have been waiting days upon days for the many moving parts of the adoption process to align so we can fly home to Colorado. I am homesick, my husband and daughters are thousands of miles away, and my dear three-year-old son and I have been one another's sole companions for almost two weeks.

It poured all afternoon. We needed to get out to the mall since we'd been cooped up in our hotel room all day. Now we are returning, and finally, the downpour has diminished. The city smells are mixed with something clean from the after-rain.

The clouds seem to want a break from filling up Colombia's skies. It is almost always cloudy here, and perhaps that's why the sight of a star thrills my little boy.

"Una estrella!" he shouts, pointing his finger upward and jumping up and down. My eyes trace the path from his finger to the sky, and I see the bright blue star he's referencing. Wait.

I get my bearings as a few other stars are in view. There's the Big Dipper…follow the arc to Arcturus and speed on to…

Spica.

And I'm lost in Spica's orbit again. The binary star system that is so close together the two stars appear as one, here again, Jesus is bringing it to my view. He and I circling each other as one. I am suddenly aware of the significance of where I am, Colombian earth beneath my feet, and who I'm with—my son.

Did I say that right? After COVID delayed our adoption process for over a year? After staring at his picture on my fridge for eighteen months, I'm really here with this child? In contrast to the heights of hope I allowed myself when I believed Elliot would come home, my hope has been a little sinking ribbon inside me for a year and a half waiting for this little boy. I didn't let myself believe, couldn't let myself believe Little J would really come home. But it finally happened. Sylvia, Valerie, and Elliot have a brother: Joncarlo. And this cherished little boy saw Spica as the first star we've viewed together.

Can it really be that God has never forgotten me? Never left me?

My little boy and I kick his soccer ball in the courtyard while the glittering stars shine overhead. We amble to the elevators, and I steal one last glance at Spica.

Blog Post: "My Sons"

Four years and three months after

Which part of your child's face is your favorite to study? You know what I mean. When he's still (for two seconds), when she's sleeping, when laughter alights their faces? I love Valerie's freckles, sprinkled across her nose like stardust. I adore Sylvia's sweet little cheeks; there's something of the baby I carried still there. Joncarlo's eyes truly stop traffic. Have there ever been such beautiful big, brown eyes? I could stare at my children's faces all day. Unless said children are whining. Then I get coffee.

I have previously chronicled the injustice of studying Elliot's face only in pictures, now four years old. I can't picture a four-year-old him. I have no concept of how he might appear in heaven. My gift is the pictures captured during his days of life on this earth, both the ultrasound and pregnancy pictures of his days inside my womb and the dozens of photos from his five days outside. In these images, I see his brow like Sylvia's, his lips like Valerie's, and his innocence like Joncarlo's.

The year and a half of being "pregnant" with the adoption process of Joncarlo created a world of suspense I am relieved to be finished with. It was no small task to get out of bed each day, holding the tension between raising my daughters, grieving a son who had died, and pursuing a son who was waiting. I felt no certainty, no "peace," that Joncarlo would come home (especially in light of COVID), only a heavy hope that it would be so.

And thank God, it is so.

Now that he is home, the shock is beginning to wear off, and many realities are beginning to set in. Our family dynamic is forever changed. A new little person (with a big personality) impacts each of us in different ways. Sylvia loves playing with him but is not so keen on extra noise, so she's allowing herself more alone time in her room. Valerie's intense emotions manifest as joy when she and her brother chase and pretend and fierce jealousy and grief when she's feeling forgotten. Dustin and I recall our days as foster parents when another child in our home similarly caused a season of simultaneous stress and delight. But this child, our son, gets to stay for good.

And our little Joncarlo. I imagine sometimes what it's like to be inside his mind, having experienced all this from the view of those big brown eyes. Being dressed on May 13 by his foster mother, the only mother he had ever known, then being taken to a neutral child welfare building and put into my arms. What could that have been like? And all the days since? Days of being carted on airplanes, in hotels, restaurants, meetings, paperwork, and doctors. The transition of arriving in Colorado and learning the sights and smells and strange expectations of a new family and new home. The absolute grief he must feel but can't articulate at leaving his foster family and never seeing them again. Even with all the empathy that I can muster, I cannot truly comprehend what my little boy's heart has endured.

And with these children and changes bouncing around me, my Elliot feels far. It's been a part of parenting I could never have understood without experiencing it—this parenting path of loving my child who has died. Elliot has never ceased being my son. In all the hustle and immense learning curve of this new season, I don't know how next to honor my beautiful, deeply missed little boy.

Last week, his precious legacy, however, stared me in the face. Joncarlo's complex medical needs necessitate a journey of referrals to specialists, scans and lab work, and eventual surgeries and therapies. I thought about this hard as we decided to pursue his adoption. We are still in the same network of doctors' offices and hospitals we utilized during all five of my pregnancies and three losses, and I knew that triggers could await me at every turn. But I knew as an adult it was my responsibility to face these triggers for the sake of a child needing excellent medical care.

But that doesn't make the triggers easy. For one appointment recently, I took Joncarlo to get an ultrasound of his kidney (he has something called a horseshoe kidney). I didn't expect it to be hard. But the ultrasound room. The hum of the machine. The exact same "ding" as the ultrasound tech took pictures. I was suddenly transported to the ultrasound appointment that changed everything, which I believe directly contributed to Elliot's death. If you've experienced trauma and know what a trigger is like, you know there's no getting out of it. There's just getting through it.

I drove home in the murk of tears, dreading an even more intense set of triggers likely to come for Joncarlo's next appointment. The next day would be Joncarlo's first appointment with the pediatric orthopedic doctor for an assessment of his radial club hand. The orthopedic department of Kaiser is in an office building downtown, across the street from St. Joseph's Hospital.

I have not been back to St. Joe's in some time. It is not normalized for me. It is the site of the most beautiful days of having Elliot in my womb and lying in a hospital bed for fifty days on bed rest, trying to save him. Those were the days of hopeful expectation and childlike trust that he would be fine. I can still feel his kick patterns if I close my eyes and allow my heart the painful gift of remembrance. Those were the innocent days of him and me surviving his traumatic birth, the joy of gazing on his perfect face, and the privilege of holding his precious hands in his incubator.

That place, that beautiful, awful place, is where reality ripped in two—the moment my son died. And reality has not mended since.

I texted my husband after the ultrasound appointment and told him I could not go downtown by myself the following day. And he understood. He always understands better than anyone because, of course, Elliot is his son, too.

Dustin immediately informed his supervisor he'd need to leave for a few hours the next day to accompany Joncarlo and me to an appointment. On the day of the appointment, as he drove us and we approached the streets leading to St. Joe's, I almost thought I would be okay. But as soon as we made that final turn and St. Joseph's Hospital came into view, any illusion of okay dissolved. My heart raced, my breathing quickened, and I felt the panic of losing Elliot rise in me as if I could somehow still save him. I don't know if there are words to describe it adequately. I still somehow want to save him.

All the worst fear of losing a child and all the ridiculous wrongness of that fear coming true returned at the sight of that building. Every feeling and memory flooded my body. That's the thing about trauma triggers. You don't just get triggered in your mind; you get triggered in your entire body. Thankfully, with Dustin there, with a job to do for the sake of Joncarlo, I was able to experience the overwhelming intensity of that moment, then find myself in the present again.

Joncarlo is quite intoxicating to look at. He gets a lot of stares, and it's less about his radial club hand and more about the reality of his being the cutest boy on the planet (not biased). There is something about him. The x-ray technician noticed this as he complied with every stance and position that she needed to x-ray his hands, arms, and spine. "He's just so sweet!" she'd declare over and over to this proud mama. "Look at those eyes!" And then, as we finished the final x-ray, she spoke to Joncarlo:

"You have such a beautiful soul. You're going to change the world." She told me that just being with him had made her day.

Wow. What was that?

After a positive meeting with the orthopedic doctor, we exited and began to drive away. The sight of St. Joe's didn't attack me with as much force the second time. In fact, something touched me in my heart, where Elliot lives in me, in the deep places Jesus guards tenderly.

I realized I had both my sons with me that day.

The doctor's office, where Joncarlo will need the most care, sits across from the site of my other son's brief earthly life. The profound meaning of this fact showed me Elliot's face the way I see my living children's faces every day. Though part of me hates how I will be forced to endure this trigger many times, the other part intuitively knows the truth.

Elliot's influence in my life directed me to Joncarlo.

I've chronicled elsewhere my derision with the theological line of thinking that God somehow intended Elliot's death, and I especially throw up a little with the idea that Elliot dying was to bring about Joncarlo's adoption into our family. That progression of thought is not only fallacious thinking of God but belittles the value of both boys. God's plan is life, and therefore Elliot's death was a sad tragedy God did not plan nor want for our family. And the God I know could have easily directed our hearts to Joncarlo with Elliot still here with us. You can debate that with me if you want, but I wouldn't recommend it. I will go full mama bear.

But God is magic at taking the worst pain and tragedy of our fallen world and bringing beauty and meaning from it. I tell you, the first time I saw Joncarlo's file, none of his medical needs scared me. All I could think was, "I would have done this and more for Elliot." Elliot's needs may have been very severe with his underdeveloped lungs, with the amount of time he may have needed in the NICU. But I would have done it, as you would for your child.

And yet more than simply being a perspective-bearer on medical needs, Elliot was somehow very involved in the decision to adopt Joncarlo. We seriously considered what Joncarlo in our family would mean for our lives and for his life. We thought about it and talked about it for months. It may sound mystical or a little contrived, but as I'd spend time in contemplative prayer, which often led to laying my wounded mama's heart to God, I'd cry for Elliot, but I'd see Joncarlo's face. I'd just, I don't know how to put it…I loved Joncarlo with a mother's love. Before I even knew he was going to be my son. The two boys felt connected to me. It was like Elliot was rooting for me, saying, "Yes, Mom, that is my little brother! Go for it!"

It might sound crazy. But it's how it happened.

So, we went for it, putting in our letter of intent for Joncarlo right after Elliot's third birthday. Little did we know, due to COVID, it would be another entire year before we'd get to Joncarlo. The timing of his official adoption decree in Colombia coming through three days before Elliot's fourth birthday, flying home with him the day after the anniversary of Elliot's death—the significance of how the days lined up is not lost on me.

And so, as I drove away from St. Joe's after Joncarlo's appointment, the reality hit me that Joncarlo is here, in many ways, because of Elliot. That little, sweet baby boy who lived just five days outside of my womb is, like the nurse said of Joncarlo, "changing the world." And the beautiful soul inside of Joncarlo that she could so clearly see? I think it is shared by my sons. I think they are brothers in a way we'll only fully understand in eternity.

I wish they were growing up together, side by side. Joncarlo's precious presence does not fill the absence of Elliot. Sometimes it amplifies just exactly what we're missing by not having Elliot here. But deep in my heart, I know Elliot is here, albeit not in the way I desire. Each time I drive to the orthopedist with Joncarlo, I'm sure I'll look at St. Joe's through streams of tears. My tears will be both bitter regret that Elliot died in that place and overwhelming privilege to care for Joncarlo's needs in a place nearby. My heart deeply grieves that Elliot did not come home. And my heart rejoices that Joncarlo did. Never can I separate these two stories because they are one story: the story of my sons.

***

In a Moment

It can be so easy to erase hard moments or seasons with time. Letting the river of days and months and years take painful memories downstream as if they never happened can be easier. And while I do think time is God's gift to soothe the acute sting of grief, trauma, and loss, I don't think time should erase all the ache.

My aching helps me stay awake to the aches of others. It is the "groaning inwardly" Paul talks about (Romans 8:23) that hurts but pushes me forward. It erases the illusion that life should be easy. Life should be a constant messy mix of the divine fingerprint in us all mingled with the sin-stained wreck of us all. The ache makes me crave eternity's perfection and gives me patience through mortality's groans.

One such area of the blessing-burden tension of this life is parenting. Isn't parenting a crazy ride? It's an innocent pursuit in your twenties or thirties to have your first baby, but none of us have a clue who that little bundle will turn out to be. Every day the love and joy my kids feel toward me and I feel toward them is tested by attitudes, selfishness (not just theirs), and disappointments. We cycle through big and small tensions sometimes hourly to hopefully arrive back at the pinnacle of tender affection. But sometimes we go to bed mad at each other, and I grieve that my little ones are growing up so fast.

When we went to Colombia to adopt Joncarlo, nerves of fear and excitement permeating our very pores, we were relieved to have the waiting time over. Our first few days in Colombia involved settling in, paperwork in Bogotá, and flying to the city of Pasto, where Joncarlo had spent his entire life. We woke the morning of May 13, day of Encuentro, of meeting our new son, with four American stomachs tied in knots. Valerie said to Dustin that morning with bittersweet wisdom, "Dad, I feel like life will never be the same again."

And she was right. A few hours later, we four waited in a large, impersonal room. Joncarlo walked in slowly and reservedly. He wore a bowtie and red blazer and clutched two of his favorite cars. What a moment, for all of us. I don't know if there is quite as profound of a metaphor for the journey that we are all on in life. Joncarlo was being taken from the family he knew, what he loved, and passing through a portal to a new family, new love. But the middle space was fear, pain, trauma, and unknowing. His own dark night.

Tension lived in us all in that moment. Of course, Sylvia and Valerie longed to bring Joncarlo home, cute as he was as a picture on our fridge. But now he was face to face with them, and they didn't know how to interact with a stranger who spoke a different language. Dustin didn't know if Joncarlo would appreciate dad hugs, so he remained close but with distance. I didn't know if I was talking too much or too little, and did he understand my Spanish? Suddenly the dream was real and, as Valerie had said, all of us knew life would never be the same. It's a shock to see your dreams come true but know in that moment you are losing a life to which you were accustomed.

Hours later, Sylvia and Joncarlo played on the see-saw at the park. He and Valerie took turns tickling each other and giggling. Dustin and the girls flew back to Colorado a few days later while I remained in Colombia for two more weeks with Joncarlo to complete adoption paperwork.

Finally, the morning came to fly home to Colorado through rushed, stressful processes to receive his visa and not miss our flight. We flew to Florida, struggled through slow responses at the immigration desk, then rushed to make our flight to Denver. Our last leg of the journey! I really did not let myself relax until we were flying to Colorado. Up until that very moment, my previous trauma told me it could all still go wrong. And it could have; some adoptive families have experienced such nightmares. But finally, flying to Colorado felt like bringing my baby home from the hospital.

Maybe my little boy sensed my relief and relaxation. After playing some tablet games and eating snacks on our final flight, Joncarlo snuggled his head onto my lap and feel hard asleep. I wonder if all the excitement, grief, fear, nerves, and joy of the past several weeks had caught up with him. He did not wake when the plane landed, nor when I put him in his stroller, nor when I put him in our van to drive home. He stayed asleep through all of it. He slept still as we took him out of the van and placed him in his new bed.

And when he woke the next morning, he was *home*. He gazed at everything in his new house with the widest smile you've ever seen. His car table, his new play kitchen, his little pizza toy and scooter bike! But more than that, here were his sisters, his mom and dad, his forever family.

Has life been simple since then? Oh, good gravy, no. Discussing the effects of adoption grief and trauma on a child and a family would take another book. We have had extremely hard days, weeks, and months. But we're in it with him just as we're with Sylvia as she becomes a tween and Valerie as she feels the aches of friendship and with family members as they struggle with health issues and with friends as they face personal hardship. Christ has been in it with all of us in every cell of each of our losses and pains even when, *especially* when, we couldn't feel him there.

If you're lost, if you're aching, if you're encased in a dark night and feel nothing, know that's probably right where Christ is holding you. You can push against him. He can take it. You can rail against your suffering. He suffers with you. You can weep. He's not telling you to dry your eyes but rather grabbing you a tissue, like my foster son did all those years ago. When you finally relax into his embrace enough to feel again, maybe, like me, you'll look back on those dark nights and realize his light was with you the whole time.

Take heart.

Afterword

Though I intentionally started putting my thoughts together in book format three years ago, it's been an almost six-year process. Six years since my beautiful Elliot grew in my womb, the last time the miracle of pregnancy was mine. As I've taken months and years to chronicle this journey, read, edit, re-read, and revise, I never feel a sense of completeness with this book. As I read the words that I wrote from year one, year two, year three, I feel differently now than I do then. But that's why I don't want to edit or remove those words; the me of those moments matters. I'm sure I will read these words in five or ten years and feel differently yet again. So how do I conclude?

I don't have a neat "ending" to wrap it all up with. Yes, I have gone from childlike certainty that I understood God, to hating him, to disbelieving in him, to numbness toward him, to slow, patient acceptance that he loves me in it all. That he loves Elliot. That he loves my other babies in heaven and the children in my home. That he loves every individual, from the polished preacher to the ragged beggar, from the forgotten child to the worshipped pop star. His love, ultimately, is all that remains when everything else is stripped away.

We finally adopted. Adopted! After so many years of that dream burning in my heart. But it's not an ending to my story with Elliot or with Jesus. Our family expanding to include Joncarlo is a sort of beginning, but isn't every day and every stage? Sylvia is becoming a young lady, and the little girl I knew is making room for a tween with such beauty and a sense of self that I don't always recognize her. I love being privileged to walk alongside her as she becomes who she is growing to be. Valerie is a friend to everyone she meets, her outward love drawing her to peers and making others feel truly special. She has a light that you'd see from a mile away. Joncarlo has been with us for almost two years, and that amazing boy has overcome incredible changes to intertwine his unique self into our family dynamic. He's learned an entirely new language, bonded with two parents and two sisters, grown physically and emotionally, and he gives this mama the best hugs and kisses.

But I'm not at the end of this journey. There are so many areas of my soul still scarred, aching, hurt, and confused. Going to church often still feels like my heart is being put in a vice, though we're dipping our toes in a new church where we're surprised to find we feel safe. Christianese statements can make my body tense with the triggers of spiritual trauma. I don't know how to sing songs with lyrics that prick at my scars or join in with ministries where God's goodness is tied to an outcome. I don't know how to answer my children's questions: "Why did God make mosquitos?!?" And when I reassure someone else of his love, but they don't feel loved, I have nothing more to say because I've been there, and some days I am still there. I cannot judge.

So how does a story like this come to an end?

I've realized that it doesn't. That's the unrealistic thing about novels with tied-up endings. The reader is left imagining a vague, hazy "ever after" without much detail and yet so much certainty. But all of us in the real world continue in the drama of life, and our outcomes are not assured.

I carry daily the dread that I could outlive more of my children. I hover to another fear that my children could lose their mom or dad to illness or accident while they are still young. Those fears, let's be honest, are more rational after experiencing the death of a child. My illusions of safety and health have been shattered. I can't pray these thoughts away. I can't say magic religious-sounding words to assure that outcome would never occur. So, I press those dreads down tightly into the space where Jesus is the sentry of my heart.

I reflect on the lessons Elliot has taught me. He reminds me to love and not judge and that every human being I meet is infinitely loved by God. My deeper acceptance of this truth has made me better for others, and I have friendships with individuals now I would have shied away from before Elliot. What a beautiful influence on me!

Elliot challenges me to seize the opportunities to make memories. Is it lavish and wasteful to spend money and time at the ocean, on camping trips, or on yearly excursions to celebrate his birthday and make memories together? Lavish? Yes! A waste? Never! Elliot taught us oh-so-heartbreakingly that we really don't know how much time we have with our loved ones. The only thing—*the only thing*—we can carry with us is our memories. We don't have to go on big vacations (though we have) to make these memories. Elliot reminds us in the walls of our home to be silly, play, dance together, and run around in the backyard. He helps us stay awake to the paramount importance of spending time together. Isn't it easy to get sidetracked from that?

But the most unyielding reflection of Elliot, and why there is no ending to this story, is the truth that this is not the end.

Throughout the first year after losing Elliot, part of my afternoon mourning ritual was to work on a slideshow video on my computer detailing his life. I selected the music which played in the background of each part of the story and each set of photographs. I played the song I wrote for him, "My Little Bird," in the background as I explained and shared pictures of his death. Then I allowed beats of silence before sharing pictures and words of living brightly in Elliot's honor. "This is Not the End" by Gungor brought the musical aspect of the video to a close.

I chose this song because these lyrics and the Scripture verses that I shared after the song reflect the one anchor of hope that allows me to move forward in life. I do not foresee that I will, in this life, have theological "answers" to the questions that still haunt me. I will never, in this life, cease aching for my Elliot. I will not, in this life, expect outcomes to demonstrate God's goodness or involvement in my life or the lives of those I love.

But this is not the end. One day, I will awake like Avery Rose in the birth story I wrote, with wider eyes that see clearly. Then I will have the only answer I'll need: Christ. Then my ache for Elliot and Avery and Everett will finally be satisfied as I embrace them for eons. Then my anxiety that more tragedy could befall my family will vanish. We will be together, breathing freely in the atmosphere of eternity.

Perhaps that all sounds like a fairy tale to you, like wishful thinking born from a broken mother's heart. I confess it might be. I have no proof to offer. Others have written volumes of the best proof, or apologetics, that can be articulated. But my own conviction is in the beautiful face of my son, whose pictures are lovingly framed and displayed around our home. I see his face, and I just know he is not truly gone. I know he exists in a way I will one day. It's the same "knowledge" that put me in Spica's orbit all those years ago: a gift of the Holy Spirit that makes us all aware there is more to life than what we see.

Life can be such a nonsensical jumble. Christian clichés and theological certainty attempt to make sense but often create more pain than they alleviate. Rest today in the humble and accommodating love of Christ. If you don't know him, take a step to know him. That can mean anything from picking up a Bible to calling a church to saying a quiet prayer to looking out your window at what he has created. He meets you in this moment, exactly where and how you are. Whatever tomorrow brings, remember that this is not the end.

> This is not the end
> This is not the end of this
> We will open our eyes wide, wider
> This is not our last
> This is not our last breath
> We will open our mouths wide, wider
> And you know you'll be alright
> Oh and you know you'll be alright
> This is not the end
> This is not the end of us
> We will shine like the stars bright, brighter.[14]

"So, we do not focus on what is seen, but what is unseen. For what is seen is temporary, but what is unseen is eternal" (2 Corinthians 4:18 NIV).

14 Gungor. "This Is Not the End." CD. *Ghosts Upon the Earth*. Michael Gungor, 2011.

References

Boyd, Gregory A. *Is God to Blame?: Moving beyond Pat Answers to the Problem of Suffering*. Readhowyouwant.com Ltd, 2011.

Boyd, Gregory. "What Is the Warfare Worldview?" Web log. *ReKnew* (blog). ReKnew, January 15, 2008. https://reknew.org/2008/01/intro-to-warfare-worldview/.

Gungor. "This Is Not the End." CD. *Ghosts Upon the Earth*. Michael Gungor, 2011.

Mae. "A Race for Our Autonomy." *3.0*. Tooth & Nail Records, 2018.

Manley Hopkins, Gerard. "Nondum [Not Yet] by Gerard Manley Hopkins." All Poetry. Accessed November 4, 2022. https://allpoetry.com/poem/13534643-Nondum--Not-yet--by-Gerard-Manley-Hopkins.

Mumford & Sons. "White Blank Page." CD. *Sigh No More*. Markus Dravs, 2008.

O'Malley, Patrick, and Tim Madigan. *Getting Grief Right: Finding Your Story of Love in the Sorrow of Loss*. Boulder, CO: Sounds True, Inc., 2017.

"Spica." Wikipedia. Wikimedia Foundation, September 2, 2022. https://en.wikipedia.org/wiki/Spica.

Starr, Mirabaii. "Dark Night of the Soul." *Mirabaii Starr, Author and Speaker* (blog). Wordpress, January 7, 2010. https://mirabaistarr.wordpress.com/2010/01/07/dark-night-of-the-soul/.

Spurgeon, Charles. "Woe and Weal." *Sermon #3239*. Speech presented at the Metropolitan Tabernacle Pulpit, March 2, 1911.

Watts, Isaac. Communion Songs. "When I Survey the Wondrous Cross." *1902 Hymnals*, n.d.

About the Author

Heidi Treibel resides in Aurora, Colorado with her husband, three children, dog, and well-stocked coffee & tea cabinet. Part of her also resides in eternity with her heaven children. Heidi has a B.A. in Education and currently writes for a local foster care agency. You can often find her gazing out the window in the hope that a blue bird might fly by. You can contact Heidi or read more of her journey at rawandfiltered.com.

www.ingramcontent.com/pod-product-compliance
Lightning Source LLC
LaVergne TN
LVHW010615100826
845148LV00014B/2977
9798988034506